Non-things

Byung-Chul Han

Non-things
Upheaval in the Lifeworld

Translated by Daniel Steuer

polity

Originally published in German as *Undinge: Umbrüche der Lebenswelt*
© by Ullstein Buchverlage GmbH, Berlin. Published in 2021 by
Ullstein Verlag

This English edition © Polity Press, 2022

Polity Press
65 Bridge Street
Cambridge CB2 1UR, UK

Polity Press
101 Station Landing
Suite 300
Medford, MA 02155, USA

ISBN-13: 978-1-5095-5169-9
ISBN-13: 978-1-5095-5170-5 (paperback)

A catalogue record for this book is available from the British Library.

Library of Congress Control Number: 2021949836

Typeset in 11pt on 15pt Janson Text
by Cheshire Typesetting Ltd, Cuddington, Cheshire
Printed and bound in Great Britain by TJ Books Ltd, Padstow,
Cornwall

The publisher has used its best endeavours to ensure that the URLs for
external websites referred to in this book are correct and active at the
time of going to press. However, the publisher has no responsibility for
the websites and can make no guarantee that a site will remain live or
that the content is or will remain appropriate.

Every effort has been made to trace all copyright holders, but if any have
been overlooked the publisher will be pleased to include any necessary
credits in any subsequent reprint or edition.

For further information on Polity, visit our website:
politybooks.com

Contents

PREFACE

In her novel *Hisoyaka na Kesshō*, the Japanese writer Yōko Ogawa tells the story of a nameless island.[1] Strange occurrences alarm its inhabitants: things disappear without explanation, and they disappear for good. Things that smell nice, and shimmering, glittering, wondrous things: hairbands, hats, perfume, small bells, emeralds, stamps – roses and birds too. And the people no longer know what all these things were once for. Along with the things, memories disappear as well.

Yōko Ogawa's novel describes a totalitarian regime whose memory police, reminiscent of Orwell's thought police, purge society of things and memories. The people live in an eternal winter of forgetfulness and loss. Anyone found to be reminiscing is arrested. The protagonist's mother, who keeps threatened things in a secret chest of drawers, and in this way protects them, is chased and killed by the memory police.

There are strong analogies between *Hisoyaka na Kesshō*, published in 1994, and our contemporary life. Today, things are also constantly disappearing, without us seeming to notice. Because the number of things has proliferated, we do not realize that, in fact, things are disappearing. In contrast to Yōko Ogawa's dystopia, we do not live in a totalitarian regime whose memory police brutally rob us of our things and memories. It is rather our intoxication by communication and information that makes things disappear. Information – that is, non-things – obscures things and drains them of their colour. We live not under a violent regime but under a rule of information that claims to be freedom.

In Ogawa's dystopia, the world is gradually emptied out. Ultimately, it disappears. Everything is seized by disappearance, by a progressive dissolution. Even body parts disappear. In the end, there are just disembodied voices aimlessly floating in the air. In many respects, the nameless island of lost things and memories resembles our present. Today's world is fading away and becoming information, information as ghostly as those disembodied voices. Digitalization de-reifies and disembodies the world. It also abolishes memory. Instead of memory, we have vast quantities of data. In the place of the memory police, we have digital media, which does its job without violence and with little effort.

Our information society is not quite as monotonous as Ogawa's dystopia. Information creates the illusion of a series of events. Information feeds off of our *attraction towards surprise*. But the attraction does not last long;

soon, there is a need for a new surprise. We are now in the habit of perceiving reality in terms of attraction and surprise. As information hunters, we are becoming blind to *still, inconspicuous things*, to *what is common, the incidental and the customary* – the things that do not attract us but *ground us in being*.

From Things to Non-things

The terrestrial order, the order of the earth, consists of things that take on a permanent form and provide a stable environment for dwelling. They are the 'things of the world', in Hannah Arendt's sense, things that 'have the function of stabilizing human life'.[1] They give stability to human life. This terrestrial order is today being replaced by the digital order. The digital order *de-reifies* the world by *informatizing* it. Decades ago, the media theorist Vilém Flusser remarked: 'Non-things are currently entering our environment from all directions, and they are pushing away the things. These non-things are called information.'[2] We are today experiencing the transition from the age of things to the age of non-things. Information, rather than things, determines the lifeworld. We no longer dwell on the earth and under the sky but on Google Earth and in the Cloud. The world is becoming

1

increasingly intangible, cloud-like and ghostly. There are no *tangible and arrestable* [*hand- und dingfest*] things.

Things stabilize human life insofar as they provide a continuity that 'lies in the fact that ... men, their ever-changing nature notwithstanding, can retrieve their sameness, that is, their identity, by being related to the same chair and the same table'.[3] Things are the calm centres of life. They have now been wholly enveloped by information. Information is anything but a calm centre of life. It is not possible to linger on information. It is relevant only fleetingly. It lives off its capacity to surprise. Information's fleetingness alone can account for the fact that information destabilizes life. It constantly attracts our attention. The tsunami of information agitates our cognitive system. Information is not a stable, uniform entity. It lacks the solidity of being. Niklas Luhmann characterizes information thus: 'Its cosmology is a cosmology not of being but of contingency.'[4]

Things are increasingly receding into the background of our attention.[5] The present hyperinflation and proliferation of things are precisely a sign of an increasing indifference towards them. We are obsessed not with things but with information and data. We now consume more information than things. We are literally becoming intoxicated with communication. Libidinal energy is redirected from things to non-things. The result is *infomania*. We are all *infomaniacs* now. Object fetishism is probably a thing of the past. We are becoming information and data fetishists. There is now even talk of 'datasexuals'.

The industrial revolution solidified and expanded the sphere of things, distancing us from nature and the crafts. But only digitalization puts an end to the paradigm of the thing. It subordinates things to information. Hardware is the subordinate base for software. Hardware is secondary compared to information; it can be made smaller and smaller. The Internet of Things turns things into information terminals. 3D printers devalue the *being* of things; things become merely the material derivatives of information.

What becomes of things when they are penetrated by information? The informatization of the world turns things into *infomatons*, that is, into information-processing *actors*. The car of the future will no longer be a thing that is associated with fantasies of power and possession, but a mobile 'centre for the distribution of information', that is, an *infomaton* that communicates with us: 'The car speaks to you, informs you "spontaneously" about its general condition – and about yours (it may refuse to function if you do not function well). It gives advice and takes decisions. It is a partner in a comprehensive negotiation over how to live.'[6]

The analysis of Dasein in Heidegger's *Being and Time* must be revised in light of the informatization of the world. Heidegger's 'being-in-the-world' involves the 'handling' of things that are either 'present-at-*hand*' or 'ready-to-*hand*'. The hand is a central figure in Heidegger's analysis of Dasein. Heidegger's 'Dasein' (the ontological name for the human being) gains access to the environment by way of the hand. Its world is a sphere of things. But today we live in an infosphere. We do not handle things that are passively given but *communicate* and *interact* with *informatons* which are themselves acting and reacting. The human being is no longer a 'Dasein' but an 'inforg' who communicates and exchanges information.[7]

In the smart home, informatons take *care* of us. They make sure everything is *cared* for. The inhabitant of a smart home is *carefree*. The telos of the digital order is probably the overcoming of that care which Heidegger takes to be the characteristic trait of human existence. *Dasein is care*. Artificial intelligence is currently busy completely de-*caring* human existence by optimizing life and doing away with the future as a source of care, that is, by overcoming *the future's contingency*. If we have a predictable future in the form of an optimized present, we need not care.

The categories of Heidegger's analysis of Dasein, such as 'history', 'thrownness' and 'facticity', all belong to the terrestrial order. Information is additive not narrative. It can be counted but not recounted. As discontinuous units that are relevant only fleetingly, information does not add up to a story. Memory is increasingly beginning to resemble a storage container in which all kinds of information are crammed. Addition and accumulation take the place of narration. History and memory are characterized by a narrative continuity that stretches across long periods of time. Meaning and coherence are founded on narration. The digital, that is, numerical, order is free of history and memory. Thus, it fragments life.

As a constantly self-reinventing, self-optimizing project, the human being rises above 'thrownness'. Heidegger's idea of 'facticity' expresses the fact that human existence is based on the non-available. Heidegger's being is another name for the non-available. 'Thrownness' and 'facticity' are part of the terrestrial order. The digital order de-facticizes human existence. It does not tolerate any non-available ground of being. The motto of the digital order is: *being is information*. All of being is therefore available and controllable. Heidegger's *thing* [*Ding*], by contrast, embodies the being-conditioned [*Be-Dingtheit*], the *facticity of human existence*. The *thing* is the *cipher* standing *for the terrestrial order*.

The infosphere is Janus-faced. It does give us more freedom, but at the same time it exposes us to more surveillance and control. Google presents the interconnected smart home of the future as an 'electronic orchestra' with the inhabitant as 'conductor'.[8] In truth, however, what the authors of this digital utopia describe is a *smart prison*. In a smart home, we are not autonomous conductors. Instead, we are *conducted* by various actors, even invisible actors that dictate the rhythm. We expose ourselves to a panoptical gaze. A smart bed fitted with various sensors continues the surveillance even during sleep. In the name of convenience, surveillance gradually creeps into everyday life. The informatons that free us from so much work turn out to be efficient *informants* that surveil and control us. In this way, we become incarcerated in the infosphere.

In a world controlled by algorithms, the human being gradually loses the power to act, loses autonomy. The human being confronts a world that resists efforts at comprehension. He or she obeys algorithmic decisions, which lack transparency. Algorithms become black boxes. The world is lost in the deep layers of neuronal networks to which human beings have no access.

Information by itself does not illuminate the world. It can even have the opposite effect. From a certain point onwards, information does not inform – it deforms. We have long since crossed this threshold. The rapid advance of informational entropy, that is, of informational chaos, pushes us into a post-factual society. The distinction between true and false is erased. Information now circulates in a hyper-real space, without any reference to reality. After all, fake news is a kind of information, and one that is possibly even more effective than facts. What counts is *short-term effect*. Effectiveness replaces truth.

Like Heidegger, Hannah Arendt holds on to the terrestrial order. She thus frequently refers to stability and duration. The things of the world stabilize human life, but so too does truth. Unlike information, truth possesses a *firmness of being*. Truth is characterized by duration and stability. *Truth* is *facticity*. It resists any change or manipulation. It thus forms the foundation of human existence: 'Conceptually, we may call truth what we cannot change; metaphorically, it is the ground on which we stand and the sky that stretches above us.'[9]

It is telling that Arendt places truth between earth and sky. Truth is a part of the terrestrial order. It gives human life *stability*. The digital order puts an end to the *age of truth* and introduces the *post-factual information society*. The post-factual regime of information elevates itself above fact-based truth. In its post-factual form, information is *thing-fleeing*. Where nothing is *arrestable*, all *stability* is lost.

Anything time-consuming is on the way out. Truth is time-consuming. Where bits of information come in quick succession, we have *no time for truth*. In our post-factual culture of excitement, communication is dominated by affects and emotions. As opposed to rationality, these are temporally unstable. They thus destabilize life. Trust, promises and responsibility are also time-consuming practices. They stretch from the present far

6

into the future. Everything that stabilizes human life is time-consuming. Faithfulness, bonding and commitment are time-consuming practices. The decay of stabilizing temporal architectures, including rituals, makes life unstable. The stabilization of life would require a *different temporal politics*.

Lingering is another time-consuming practice. Perception that latches on to information does not have a *lasting and slow gaze*. Information makes us short-sighted and short of breath. It is not possible to linger on information. Lingering on things in contemplation, intentionless seeing, which would be a formula for happiness, gives way to the hunt for information. Today, we pursue information without gaining *knowledge*. We take notice [*nehmen Kenntnis*] of everything without gaining any *insight* [*Erkenntnis*]. We travel [*fahren*] across the world without having an *experience* [*Erfahrung*]. We communicate incessantly without participating in a *community*. We collect vast quantities of data without following up on our *recollections*. We accumulate 'friends' and 'followers' without meeting an *Other*. In this way, information develops a form of life that has no stability or duration.

There can be no doubt that the infosphere has an emancipatory effect. It liberates us more effectively from the hardship of work than the sphere of things could. Human civilization can be understood as the gradual *intellectualization of reality*. Humans transfer their intellectual capacities on to things so that the things can do the work for them. In this process, subjective spirit becomes objective spirit. Things that take the form of machines represent a civilizational advance, for they contain that drive – a primitive form of spirit – which enables them

7

to act autonomously. In the *Philosophie des Geistes*, Hegel writes:

> But a tool does not yet have the activity in itself; it is an *inert* thing . . . – I still have to work with it; I have placed *cunning* between myself and the external world of things – in order to preserve myself . . . and let the tool suffer the wear and tear . . . yet, I still get blisters; making myself a thing is still a necessary moment in this; the activity of my own drive not yet in the thing. My own activity also needs to be put into the tool; it has to be made autonomously acting.[10]

Because it is not autonomously active, a tool is an inert thing. The human being handling it turns him- or herself into a thing – develops blisters on his or her hands. With automatic machines, no one gets blisters any more, but nevertheless the liberation from work is not yet complete. It is the machine that creates the factory and the worker.

The next step in the process of civilization implants not only the drive but also the intelligence, this higher form of spirit, into the thing. Artificial intelligence transforms things into informatons. The 'cunning' in this lies in the fact that human beings now have the things not just work for them but also think for them. A machine does not free the hand from work, but an informaton does. Hegel could not yet imagine artificial intelligence, however. He concentrated all too strongly on work; he did not have any access to a non-work form of life. For Hegel it was clear: *spirit is work*. *Spirit is hand*. The emancipatory effects of digitalization promise a form of life that resembles *play*. Digitalization produces *digital unemployment*, an unemployment not caused by the economic cycle.

Vilém Flusser summarizes the new, information-dominated world order as follows: 'We can no longer hold tight to things, and we do not know how to hold tight to information. There is nothing to hold on to.'[11] Although sceptical at first, Flusser eventually imagines the future in utopian pictures. The lack of anything to hold on to gives way to the hovering lightness of play. The human being of the future is no longer interested in things – is not a worker (*homo faber*) but a player (*homo ludens*). He or she no longer needs to engage in the tedious work of overcoming the resistance of material reality. Human beings of the future will program machines to do the work – they themselves will be handless: 'This new human being that is being born around us and inside us is actually handless. It no longer handles things, and one can therefore in this case no longer speak of acts [*Handlungen*].'[12]

The hand is the organ of work and action. The finger, by contrast, is the organ of choice. The handless human beings of the future only use their fingers. They *choose* rather than *act*. They push buttons in order to satisfy their needs. Their lives are not dramas in which they are compelled to act; their lives are play. They do not want to possess anything. They want only to experience and enjoy.

The handless human beings of the future closely resemble the *phono sapiens*, busy on their smartphones. Smartphones are their playgrounds. It is almost as though the human being of the future will be entirely without 'care' – will only play and enjoy. Is the increasing gamification of the lifeworld, of communication as well as of work, evidence that the age of the human being as player is already upon us? Should we welcome the playing *phono sapiens*? Nietzsche already anticipated him: 'One still works, for work is a form of entertainment . . . One has one's little pleasure for the day and one's little pleasure for the night: but one honors health.'[13]

With *phono sapiens*, who seeks only experience, enjoyment and play, we bid farewell to freedom in Hannah Arendt's sense, that kind of freedom that is tied to acting [*Hand*lung]. Whoever *acts* [*handelt*] breaks with the present and brings something new, something altogether different into the world. Someone who acts needs to overcome *resistance*. Play, by contrast, does not interfere with reality. Acting [*Handeln*] is the proper verb for history. The playing, handless human being of the future embodies the end of history.

Every age has a different definition of freedom. In antiquity, freedom meant that you were a free man, not a slave. In modernity, freedom was turned inwards and became the autonomy of the subject. It was the freedom in acting. Today, the freedom to act has been reduced to the freedom of choice and consumption. The handless human being of the future indulges in a 'freedom at one's fingertips': 'There are so many available keys that my fingertips can never touch them all. Therefore, I get the impression of being perfectly free in my decisions.'[14] This freedom at your fingertips turns out to be an illusion. Free choice [*Wahl*] is in fact *consumer choice* [*Auswahl*]. The handless human beings of the future are not presented with a *genuine choice*; they do not *act*. They live in *post-history*. They do not even notice that they no longer have hands. *We*, by contrast, still have *hands*, and are *able to act*, and so we are able to criticize. Only hands are capable of *choice*, of the freedom of acting.

A form of rule in which human beings did nothing but play would be perfect domination. Juvenal coined the phrase *panem et circenses* (bread and circuses) to characterize a Roman society in which political action had become impossible. People were sedated with free food and spectacular games. Universal basic income and computer games would be the modern *panem et circenses*.

From Possessing to Experiencing

Understood abstractly, experiencing means consuming information. Today, we prefer *experiencing* to *possessing*, *being* to *having*. Experiencing is a form of *being*. Thus, in *To Have or to Be* Erich Fromm writes: 'Having refers to *things*. . . . Being refers to *experience*.'[1] Fromm's criticism of modern society – that it focuses on having rather than being – is no longer completely apt, for we now live in a society of experiencing and communicating that prefers being to having. The old maxim of having – the more I *have*, the more I *am* – no longer holds. The new maxim of experiencing is: the more I *experience*, the more I *am*.

TV programmes such as *Cash in the Attic* well demonstrate this imperceptible change of paradigm. We painlessly, almost heartlessly, part ways with things that previously were close to our hearts. It is telling that most of the people on the programme want to use the money they receive from the 'traders' for 'travelling', as if travels were rituals of separation from things. The *memories* stored in things have suddenly lost all value; they have to give way to new *experiences*. It seems that people are no longer able to dwell with things or to imbue them with life and make them their faithful companions. Things close to our hearts presuppose an intense libidinal tie. Now, we no longer want to be tied to things or people. *Ties* are untimely. They restrict the space of possible experiences, that is, *freedom in the sense of consumption.*

We even expect the consumption of things to provide us with experiences. The informational content of things, for instance their brands, is more important than their use value. We perceive things primarily with regard to the information embedded in them. When we purchase things, we buy and consume emotions. Products are charged with emotions by way of storytelling. What determines the value added is the *distinguishing information* that promises the consumer a special experience – or even the experience of specialness. The informational aspect of a commodity becomes ever more important than its material aspect. The aesthetic-cultural content of a commodity is the actual product. The economy of experiences replaces the economy of things.

It is far more difficult to possess information than it is to possess things. This leads to the impression that information belongs to everyone. Possession relates to the paradigm of the thing. The world of information is controlled not by possession but by *access*. Attachment to things or places is replaced with temporary access to networks and platforms. The sharing economy weakens the identification with things that is at the heart of possession.

Possession [*Besitzen*] is based on being sedentary [*Sitzen*]. The constant compulsion to move makes it harder to identify with things and places. Things and places also have less and less influence on the formation of our own identities. Identity is today primarily produced through information. We *produce ourselves* on social media. The French expression *se produire* means *to play to the gallery*. We *stage ourselves*. We *perform our identities*.

For Jeremy Rifkin, the transition from possession to access is a deep paradigm shift that leads to decisive changes in the lifeworld. Rifkin even predicts the dawn of a new type of human being:

> Entry and access are the key terms of the dawning age
> ... [property's] waning significance in commerce sug-
> gests a formidable change in the way future generations
> will perceive of human nature. Indeed, a world struc-
> tured around access relationships is likely to produce a
> very different kind of human being.[2]

Human beings who are not interested in things, in possession, do not submit to the 'thing morality', which is based on work and property.[3] They prefer play to work, experiencing and enjoying to possessing. In its cultural phase, the economy also exhibits traits of playfulness. Staging and performing become increasingly important. Cultural production, that is, the production of information, increasingly adopts artistic processes. *Creativity* becomes the catchword.

In the age of non-things, there is something almost utopian about the notion of *possession*. Possession is characterized by an intimacy and inwardness. For a thing to be a possession, I must have an intense relationship with it. You do not *possess* an electronic gadget. Because we no longer *possess* them, consumer goods quickly end up on the rubbish heap. Possession is something internalized and psychologically charged. Things in my possession are vessels filled with emotions and recollections. The *history* that things acquire in the course of being used for a long time gives them souls and turns them into things close to the heart. Only *discreet things*, however, can be animated by intensive libidinal ties and become things close to the heart. Today's consumer goods are indiscreet, intrusive and over-expressive. They come loaded with prefabricated ideas and emotions that impose themselves on the consumer. Hardly anything of the consumer's life enters into them.

According to Walter Benjamin, 'ownership is the most intimate relationship that one can have to objects [*zu Dingen*]'.[4] The collector is the owner par excellence. For Benjamin, the collector is a utopian figure, a future saviour of things. His 'concern' is 'the transfiguration of things'. He

> dreams his way not only into a distant or bygone world but also into a better one – one in which, to be sure, human beings are no better provided with what they need than in the everyday world, but in which things are freed from the drudgery of being useful.[5]

In this utopian future, human beings will make an altogether different use of things, one that is no longer a *using up*. The collector, the saviour of things, commits himself to 'the Sisyphean task of divesting things

15

of their commodity character by taking possession of them'.[6] Benjamin's collector is interested not so much in the use or exchange value of things as in their history and physiognomy. In his hands, the age, landscape, craft and previous owners of the thing crystallize into a 'magic encyclopedia whose quintessence is the fate of his object'.[7] The true collector is the opposite of the consumer; collectors are 'interpreters of fate', 'physiognomists of the world of objects [*Dingwelt*]'. As soon as a collector 'holds [things] in his hands, he seems to be seeing through them into their distant past as though inspired'.[8]

Benjamin quotes the well-known Latin saying *Habent sua fata libelli* (books have their fate).[9] For Benjamin, a book has a fate insofar as it is a thing, a possession. It carries material marks that give it a history. An e-book is not a *thing*, but *information*; it has an altogether different status of being. Even if we have it at our disposal, it is not a *possession*. It is something to which we have *access*. An e-book reduces a book to informational value. The book has no age, place, craft or owner. It lacks the auratic distance from which an individual fate could speak to us. Fate has no place in the digital order. Information has neither a physiognomy nor a fate, and it does not allow for the formation of intense ties. One cannot have, for instance, a *personal* copy [*Handexemplar*] of an e-book. A personal copy of a book is given its unmistakeable face, its physiognomy, by the *hand* of the owner. E-books are faceless and without history. They may be read without the use of the *hands*. There is a tactile element in the turning of a book's pages that is constitutive of every *relationship*. Without bodily touch, no ties can emerge.

Our future will most likely not be Benjamin's utopia, in which things are divested of their character as commodities. The *time of things* is past. TV programmes such as *Cash in the Attic* reveal that, today, the things that are close to our heart are mercilessly turned into commodities. Information capitalism is an intensified form of capitalism. Unlike industrial capitalism, it commodifies not just the material world but the immaterial world. Life itself takes on the form of a commodity. Human relationships are commercialized wholesale. Social media exploits all communication. Platforms such as Airbnb commercialize hospitality. Information capitalism conquers every corner of our lives, even of our souls. Human affection is replaced with ratings or likes. Friendships are, above all else, things to be counted. All of culture becomes a commodity. Through storytelling, even the histories of places are exploited in order to produce value. Products are enriched with micro-stories. The difference between culture and commercialism is fast disappearing. Cultural sites reinvent themselves as profit-making brands.

The origin of culture lies in community. Culture teaches symbolic values that found a community. The more culture becomes a commodity, the more it leaves its origin behind. The total commercialization and commodification of culture leads to the destruction of community. The 'community' that is so frequently invoked on digital platforms is a commodified form of community. Community as a commodity spells the end of community.

Smartphone

In the early days of the telephone, this new technology had an aura of fate-like power about it. Its resounding ringing was like an order to which one had to submit. In his *Berlin Childhood around 1900*, Benjamin describes how, as a child, he was helplessly at the mercy of the apparatus:

> At that time, the telephone still hung – an outcast settled carelessly between the dirty-linen hamper and the gasometer – in a corner of the back hallway, where its ringing served to multiply the terrors of the Berlin household. When, having mastered my senses with great effort, I arrived to quell the uproar after prolonged fumbling through the gloomy corridor, I tore off the two receivers, which were heavy as dumbbells, thrust my head between them, and was inexorably delivered over to the voice that now sounded. There was nothing to

allay the violence with which it pierced me. Powerless, I suffered, seeing that it obliterated my consciousness of time, my firm resolve, my sense of duty. And just as the medium obeys the voice that takes possession of him from beyond the grave, I submitted to the first proposal that came my way through the telephone.[1]

The medium is the message. The resounding telephone in the dark corridor, with receivers as heavy as dumbbells, prefigures the message and lends it something of the uncanny. The noises of the first telephone conversations were 'nocturnal noises'.[2] The mobile phones we carry around in our pockets today do not possess the *heavy weight of fate*. They are handy and light; we literally have a grip on them. Fate is that alien power that *immobilizes* us. A message, as the *voice of fate*, does not leave us much room to manoeuvre. The *mobility* of the smartphone is enough to give us a feeling of freedom. No one is terrorized by its ringing. The smartphone does not force us into a helpless passivity. No one is delivered over to the *voice of another*.

The constant typing and swiping on the smartphone is an almost liturgical gesture, and it has a substantive impact on our relation to the world. I swipe away the information that does not interest me. I zoom in on the content that I like. I have the world firmly in my grip. The world has to accord with my desires. In this way, the smartphone amplifies self-referentiality. Through all my swiping, I submit the world to my needs. The world appears to me under the *digital illusion of total availability*.

According to Roland Barthes, the sense of touch 'is the most demystifying of all senses, unlike sight, which is the most magical'.[3] *The truly beautiful cannot be touched. It demands distance.* Faced with the sublime, we stand back in awe. When praying, we fold our hands. The sense of touch destroys distance. It knows no astonishment. It demystifies, de-auratizes and renders profane what is touched. The touchscreen sublates the *negativity of the other, of the unavailable.* It generalizes the *haptic compulsion* to make everything available. In the age of the smartphone, even the sense of sight succumbs to haptic compulsion, and loses its magic. It loses the capacity for astonishment. The distance-destroying, consuming way of seeing approximates the sense of touch. It desecrates the world. To this way of seeing, the world appears only in the form of availability. For the frantically typing index finger, everything is consumable. The index finger that orders commodities or food necessarily transfers its consumerist habitus to other areas. Everything it touches takes on the form of a commodity. On Tinder, it degrades the other, who becomes a sexual object. Deprived of his or her *otherness*, the *other* becomes consumable.

In digital communication, the *other* is increasingly absent. Smartphones allow us to retreat into bubbles that screen us off from the other. Digital communications rarely involve salutations; the other is not explicitly *addressed*. We prefer to write a text message rather than ring someone up, because in writing we are less exposed to the other. Thus, the *other as a voice* disappears.

Communication with a smartphone is disembodied and without a gaze. Community has a bodily dimension. Because of its lack of corporeality, digital communication weakens community. The gaze stabilizes community. Digitalization makes the *other as gaze* disappear. The absence of the gaze is partly responsible for the loss of empathy in the digital age. When a parent stares at a smartphone, the infant is deprived of the gaze. The gaze of the mother, in particular, provides an infant with stability, self-affirmation and community. The gaze builds primordial trust. Without the gaze, a disturbed relationship to self and others develops.

What makes a smartphone different from a conventional mobile phone is that it is not just a telephone but, primarily, a medium for transmitting images and information. The world only becomes fully available and consumable once it is reified into an image:

> 'Picture' means . . . that which sounds in the colloquial expression to be 'in the picture' about something. . . . To 'put oneself in the picture' about something means: to *place* the being itself before one just as things are with it, and, as so *placed*, to keep it permanently before one.[4]

The smartphone *places* the world: it *takes hold* of it by placing [her*stellen*] it in front of us in the form of an image. The camera and the screen are the central elements of the smartphone because they intensify the *becoming-image of the world*. Digital images transform the world into *available information*. The smartphone is a '*Ge-Stell*', enframing, in Heidegger's sense: a *Gestell*, the essence of technology, unites in itself all forms of *placing* [*Stellens*] that make available, such as ordering [*Bestellen*], presenting [*Vorstellen*] or producing [*Herstellen*]. The next step in the process of civilization goes beyond the becoming-image of the world. It consists of the production of the world *out of images*, the production, that is, of a *hyper-real reality*.

21

The world consists of things as objects. The word 'object' is derived from the Latin verb *obicere*, which means 'set against', 'throw against' or 'oppose'. The negativity of resistance is inherent in it. An object is something that turns against me, that opposes and resists me. Digital objects lack the negativity of *obicere*. I do not experience them as resistance. The smartphone is smart because it deprives reality of its character as resistant. Even the smooth surface of the smartphone conveys the sense of a lack of resistance. On its smooth touchscreen, everything seems tame [*handzahm*] and obliging. Everything is available at the tip of one's fingers. The smartphone's smooth surface is a *digital flatterer* that *blandishes the hand* and thus constantly elicits '*likes*' from us. Digital media may be effective in overcoming the resistance of space and time, but it is precisely the *negativity of resistance* that constitutes *experience*. The smart environment of digital non-resistance impoverishes world and experience.

The smartphone is the main informaton of our time. It not only makes many things superfluous but also de-reifies the world by reducing it to information. The material aspect of the smartphone recedes, and information takes its place; the materiality of the smartphone is not perceived in its own right. Smartphones do not really differ in their appearance. We look *through them* into the infosphere. An analogue watch also provides us with information regarding time, but it is not an informaton; it is a thing, even an *adornment*. Its material aspect is central to it.

A society that is dominated by information and informatons is *unadorned*. Adornment [*Schmuck*] originally meant *splendid attire*. Non-things are naked. The decorative and the ornamental are characteristic of things. They are life's way of telling us that life is about more than mere functioning. In the baroque age, the ornamental was *theatrum dei*, the theatre of the gods. If we submit life fully to functionality and information, we drive the divine out of life. The smartphone is a symbol of our time. The smartphone is not *embellished* in any way. It is dominated by the *smooth* and *straight*. Even the communication that takes place via smartphones lacks the *magic of beautiful forms*. It is dominated by a *straightforwardness* that finds its best expression in *affects*. The smartphone also intensifies hypercommunication: everything is levelled out, abraded and ultimately made to conform [*gleichgeschaltet*]. We may live in a 'society of singularities', but paradoxically the singular, the incomparable, is hardly to be found.

We present our smartphones everywhere, and even delegate our perception to these apparatuses. We perceive reality through the filter of the screen. The digital window dilutes reality into information that we *register*. There is no *physical contact* with reality. Reality is deprived of its *presence*. We no longer perceive the *material vibrations* of reality. Perception is disembodied. The smartphone de-realizes the world.

Things do not spy on us. This is why we *trust* them. The smartphone, by contrast, is not only an informaton but also a very efficient informant that keeps its user under constant surveillance. Anyone familiar with its internal algorithmic life will rightly feel tracked by it. We are controlled and programmed by it. It is not we who use the smartphone; the smartphone uses us. The real actor is the smartphone. We are at the mercy of this digital informant, beneath the surface of which various actors steer and distract us.

The emancipatory aspects of the smartphone are not all there is to it. There is no fundamental difference between being reachable at all times and being enslaved. The smartphone is a mobile labour camp in which we voluntarily intern ourselves. The smartphone is also a *pornophone*: we voluntarily expose ourselves. The smartphone functions like a mobile confessional box. It is the continuation of the 'sacral rule of the confessional box' in another form.[5]

Every form of rule has its own devotional objects. The theologian Ernst Troeltsch speaks of 'devotional objects that fascinate the imagination of the people'.[6] These objects stabilize rule by making it habitual and anchoring it in the body. In German, *devot* also means submissive. Smartphones have established themselves as the devotional objects of the neoliberal regime. As apparatuses that serve the purpose of submission, they resemble the rosary, which is just as mobile and handy. The *like* is the digital amen. By clicking on the like button, we submit ourselves to the context of rule.

Platforms like Facebook or Google are our new feudal lords. We tirelessly work their land and produce the valuable data that they exploit. We feel free, although we are completely exploited and controlled. In a system that exploits freedom, there is no resistance. Once it coincides with freedom, rule becomes total.

At the end of her *The Age of Surveillance Capitalism*, Shoshana Zuboff invokes collective resistance, pointing to the fall of the Berlin Wall:

The Berlin Wall fell for many reasons, but above all it was because the people of East Berlin said, 'No more!' We too can be the authors of many 'great and beautiful' new facts that reclaim the digital future as humanity's home. No more! Let this be *our* declaration.[7]

The communist system that *represses* freedom differs fundamentally from the neoliberal surveillance capitalism that *exploits* freedom. We are too intoxicated by our digital drugs, by communication, to raise the voice of resistance and cry 'No more!'. There is simply no place here for any romantic notion of revolution. The conceptual artist Jenny Holzer's remark 'Protect Me From What I Want' expressed a truth that Zuboff apparently failed to appreciate.

The neoliberal regime is itself smart. Smart power does not operate through orders or prohibitions. It does not make us docile; it makes us dependent and addicted. Instead of breaking our wills, it serves our needs. It wants to be liked. It is permissive rather than repressive. It does not condemn us to silence. Rather, we are constantly asked to share our opinions, preferences, needs and desires – even to tell the stories of our lives. Smart power conceals its intention to rule by coming across as friendly, smart. The subject is not even aware of its submission. It believes that it is free. Capitalism culminates in the capitalism of the like. Because it is permissive, it need not fear resistance or revolution.

Our almost symbiotic relationship with our smartphones has led some to suggest that they represent transitional objects, the term coined by the psychoanalyst Donald Winnicott to refer to those things that secure an infant's safe passage towards reality. Only with the help of transitional objects can the infant create a play area, an 'intermediate area',[8] in which it 'relaxes as in a secure and uncontested resting place'.[9] Transitional objects build a bridge to reality, to the other, to what escapes the fantasy of omnipotence. Young infants will grasp at the corner of a blanket or cushion, to put it in their mouth or to stroke. Later, they grasp a complete object, such as a doll or cuddly toy. Transitional objects have an existential function. They give the child a feeling of security. They take away the fear of being alone. The create trust and a feeling of being sheltered. Transitional objects allow children to slowly grow into the world. They are the *first things of the world* which stabilize the life of the infant.

A child has a very intense, deep relationship with the transitional object. The object must be neither modified nor washed. Nothing is allowed to interrupt the experience of closeness. The child panics if it loses the beloved object. The child possesses the transitional object, but to a certain extent it also has a life of its own. It appears as an independent, personal counterpart to the child. Transitional objects open up a *dialogical space* in which the child can encounter the *other*.

We react with uncontrollable panic when we lose our smartphones. We have intimate relationships with them. We do not like to give them to other people. Can the smartphone therefore be understood as a transitional object, a digital teddy bear? The fact that the smartphone is a narcissistic object suggests not. A transitional object represents the *other*. The child speaks to it, cuddles it, as if it were another person. No one cuddles a smartphone. No one perceives it as an independent counterpart.

Unlike a transitional object, it is not something close to our heart; it is not irreplaceable. We regularly buy new smartphones.

The way the child plays with the transitional object is analogous to later creative activities, for instance in the arts. It opens up a free space. The child, as though in a dream, takes the position of the transitional object; it gives free rein to its fantasies. The child imbues the transitional object with symbolic value. The object becomes the vessel in which the child's dreams are concentrated. The smartphone, by contrast, floods us with stimuli and represses our imagination. Transitional objects are *poor in stimuli* and therefore intensify and structure attention. The flood of stimuli that comes from the smartphone fragments our attention. Where the transitional object stabilizes the psyche, the smartphone destabilizes it.

Transitional objects create a *relationship with the other*. Our relationship with the smartphone, by contrast, is narcissistic. The smartphone is similar in many ways to a so-called 'autistic object'. We could also call it a narcissistic object. Transitional objects are *soft*. The child snuggles up to them. When doing so, it feels not itself but the *other*. Autistic objects are hard: 'The hardness of the object allows the child, when manipulating and pressing the object, to feel not so much the object but itself.'[10] Autistic objects lack the *dimension of the other*. They do not fuel our fantasying. Our dealings with them are repetitive, not creative. *Repetitiveness* and *compulsion* characterize our relationship to the smartphone.

Like transitional objects, autistic objects are a substitute for the absent person, but they reify this person into an *object*. They take away the person's *otherness*:

Autistic objects are the most extreme example of objects taking the place of human beings, even of serving the purpose of avoiding the imponderables and always possible separations that are an inevitable part of relations with autonomously acting human beings. To put it even more radically: they make it possible not to perceive others as independent human beings at all.[11]

The similarity between smartphones and autistic objects is obvious. Unlike the transitional object, the smartphone is *hard*; it is not a digital teddy bear. Rather, it is a narcissistic, autistic object through which we *feel*, most of all, *ourselves*. It thus also destroys empathy. We use the smartphone to retreat into a narcissistic sphere in which we are protected against the *imponderables pertaining to the other*. The smartphone puts the other *at our disposal* by reifying the other into an object. It turns the *you* into an *it*. The *disappearance of the other* is the ontological reason why the smartphone makes us lonely. We communicate so compulsively, so excessively, because we are lonely and empty. But hypercommunication is not fulfilling. Because it lacks the *presence of the other*, it only deepens the loneliness.

Selfies

An analogue photo is a *thing*. We take great care to keep it safe, as we do with all things close to our heart. Because of its material nature, it is fragile and exposed to the processes of ageing and decay. It is born and dies: 'like a living organism, it is born on the level of the sprouting silver grains, it flourishes a moment, then ages . . . Attacked by light, by humidity, it fades, weakens, vanishes.'[1] Analogue photography also embodies the transience of the referent. The photographed object inexorably recedes into the past. Photography *mourns*.

The drama of death and resurrection rules over Barthes's theory of photography, which can be read as a paean to analogue photography. As a fragile thing, a photograph is destined to die, but at the same time photography is a medium of resurrection. It captures the rays of light coming from its referent and preserves them on silver grains. It does not just bring back memories of the dead. By letting them come *alive* again, it also makes possible an *experience of presence*. Photography is an 'ectoplasm', a magic 'emanation of *past reality*', a mysterious alchemy of immortality: 'the loved body is immortalized by the mediation of a precious metal, silver (monument and luxury); to which we might add the notion that this metal, like all the metals of Alchemy, is alive'.[2] Photography is the umbilical cord that connects the beholder to the loved body beyond its death. It achieves the loved body's resurrection and saves it from death. Thus, photography 'has something to do with resurrection'.[3]

Barthes's *Camera Lucida* is the result of a profound work of mourning. The author invokes, with great intensity, his dead mother. Of a photograph of his mother that is not reproduced in the book (*it is conspicuous by its absence*), he writes: 'Hence the Winter Garden Photograph, however pale, is for me the treasury of rays which emanated from my mother as a child, from her hair, her skin, her dress, her gaze, *on that day*.'[4] Barthes capitalizes 'Photograph', as if it were a formula for redemption, even a code word for resurrection.

The experience of the fragility of human life, which is intensified by photography, creates a need for redemption. Agamben thus also links photography to the idea of resurrection, calling photography a 'prophecy of the glorious body'.[5] The subject of a photograph emits a 'mute address', a 'demand for redemption':[6]

the subject shown in the photo demands something of us. . . . Even if the person photographed is completely forgotten today, even if his or her name has been erased

30

forever from human memory – or, indeed, precisely because of this – that person and that face demand their name; they demand not to be forgotten.[7]

The *angel of photography* continually renews the promise of resurrection. It is the angel of recollection and redemption. It lifts us above the fragility of life.

Analogue photography transfers the traces of light coming from the object, via the negative, on to paper. The analogue photograph is an *image of light*. The light is reborn in the darkroom: the darkroom is in fact a *bright room*. The digital medium, by contrast, transforms the rays of light into data, that is, into numeric relations. Data is *without light*. It is *neither bright nor dark*. Data interrupts the *light* of life. The digital medium interrupts the magic relation in which the object is connected to photography via the light. An 'analogue' is something that is similar. Chemistry is an analogue of light. The rays of light coming from an object are preserved in silver grains. There is, by contrast, no similarity between light and numbers. The digital medium *translates* light into data. In this process, the light is lost. In digital photography, alchemy gives way to mathematics. It disenchants photography.

Analogue photography is a 'certificate of presence'.[8] It testifies to the 'That-has-been'.[9] It is *in love with reality*: 'The only thing that interests me about a photograph is the fact that it shows something that exists, that I see in it no more and no less than "so this actually exists!"'[10] If the 'That-has-been' is the truth of photography, digital photography is *pure illusion*. Digital photography is *not an emanation but an elimination of the referent*. Digital photography does not have an intense, libidinal attachment to the object. It does not immerse itself in the object, does not fall in love with it. It does not *call upon* it, does not enter into a *dialogue* with it. It is not based on a singular, unique, irrevocable encounter with the object. The seeing itself is delegated to the apparatus. The possibilities of digital post-processing weaken the connection with the referent. They make it impossible to *abandon oneself to reality*. De-coupled from the referent, the photograph becomes self-referential. Artificial intelligence generates a new, expanded reality that *does not exist*, a hyper-reality that no longer corresponds to reality, to a real referent. Digital photography is hyper-real.

As a medium of recollection, analogue photography tells a *story*, a destiny. It is surrounded by a *novel-like* horizon:

> The date belongs to the photograph . . . because it makes me lift my head, allows me to compute life, death, the inexorable extinction of the generations: it is *possible* that Ernest, a schoolboy photographed in 1931 by Kertész, is still alive today (but where? how? What a novel!).[11]

Digital photography is not *novel-like* but episodic. Smartphones create a kind of photography with an altogether different temporality, one without temporal depth, without novel-like breadth, a photography without destiny or recollection, that is, an *instantaneous photography*.

Walter Benjamin pointed out that, in photography, exhibition value increasingly pushes aside cult value. Cult value, however, does not withdraw without offering some resistance. The 'human countenance' is its last 'entrenchment'. Thus, the portrait is at the centre of early photography. Cult value lives on in the 'cult of remembrance of dead or absent loved ones'. The 'fleeting expression of a human face' creates the aura that gives photography its 'melancholic and incomparable beauty'.[12]

The human countenance is today again conquering photography – in the form of the selfie. The selfie turns the countenance into a *face*, which is then exhibited on digital platforms such as Facebook. Unlike the analogue portrait, the selfie is bursting at the seams with exhibition value. Cult value disappears altogether. A selfie is an exhibited face without aura. It lacks 'melancholic' beauty. It is characterized by *digital cheerfulness*.

The essence of the selfie is not exhausted by narcissism alone. What is novel about the selfie concerns its *status of being*. A selfie is not a *thing*; it is *information*, a *non-thing*. Non-things supplant things: this is also true of photography. The smartphone makes *photographic things* disappear. The validity of selfies, as information, is limited to digital communication. Along with photographic things, recollection, destiny and history are also disappearing.

Barthes's photograph of his mother is a thing, even a thing close to his heart. It is a pure expression of her as a person. She *is* the mother. On this photograph, the mother is present *as a thing*. The photograph *embodies* her presence. As a thing close to the heart, the photograph remains outside of communication. Exhibition would destroy it. That is the exact reason why Barthes does not reproduce the photograph in his book, despite incessantly talking about it. Its essence is that of a *secret*. The term *arcanum* points to a box (*arca*). Barthes's photograph is kept in a box, amid *odds and ends* even, like a secret. If it were shown to others, it would immediately lose its magic. Its owner keeps it exclusively *for himself*.

This *for-oneself* is alien to the character of selfies and other digital photos. They are visual communications, pieces of *information*. Taking a selfie is a communicative act. They *must* be exposed to the view of others, *must* be shared. Their essence is *exhibition*, whereas the character of a photograph is that of a *secret*.

Selfies are not made to be kept. They are not a medium of recollection. For this reason, no one makes prints of them. Like all information, selfies are tied to the actual moment. *Repetition* would be pointless. Selfies are acknowledged only once. After that, their status of being is like that of an answerphone message to which one has already listened. The digital communication of images de-reifies them into pure information. The messaging platform Snapchat, which deletes photos after a few seconds, does perfect justice to the character of the selfie. Selfies have the same temporality as oral communication. Even the other sorts of photos that people take with smartphones are treated like information. They no longer have anything thing-like about them. Their status of being differs fundamentally from that of analogue photographs. The analogue photograph is more a monument than a snapshot.

Snapchat represents the culmination of *instantaneous digital communication*. It embodies the time of the digital in its purest form. *The moment is all that counts*. A Snapchat 'story' is not a *story* in the proper sense. It is not narrative but additive – no more than a list of snapshots. Digital time disintegrates into a mere sequence of point-like presences. It has no *narrative continuity*. It thus transforms life itself into something fleeting. Digital objects do not permit any *lingering*. In this way, they differ from things.

Selfies are characterized by playfulness, and digital communication generally has something playful about it. Communication becomes a playground for *phono sapiens*. *Phono sapiens* is more *homo ludens* than *homo faber*. Visual communication through digital photography is far better suited to playing and acting than is written communication.

As selfies are primarily messages, they have a tendency to be over-expressive. Extreme postures are common. There are no mute selfies. Analogue portraits, by contrast, are usually *quiet*. They do not demand one's attention. This *quietness* is precisely what gives them their expressive force. Selfies are loud, but poor in genuine expression. Because of the exaggerated postures affected, the subjects look like masks. The fact that visual digital communication has taken hold of the human face is not without consequence. The face has taken on the *form of a commodity*. As Benjamin would say, the face has irrevocably lost its *aura*.

Analogue portraits are a kind of *still life*. They are meant to express the *person* they depict. When we are in front of a camera, we are therefore very eager to make sure that the picture corresponds to us. We want the picture to approximate our inner picture of ourselves, so we feel our way towards this inner picture. We pause. We turn inwards. For this reason, analogue portraits often have an air of seriousness. The postures adopted are restrained. Selfies, by contrast, do not testify to the person. The use of standardized facial expressions, such as 'duckface', precludes any attempt at personal expression. With tongue stretched out and one eye closed, each of us looks the same. We *play to the gallery*; that is, we *stage* ourselves in different postures and roles.

The selfie announces the disappearance of the kind of human being who is burdened by destiny and history. It expresses a form of life that devotes itself playfully to the moment. *Selfies do not mourn.* Death and transience are fundamentally alien to the selfie. *Funeral selfies* – I am thinking of those selfies taken at funerals in which people smile happily at the camera, next to a coffin – reflect an absence of mourning. A grinning *I am* is projected at death. This we might call the *digital work of mourning*.

Artificial Intelligence

On a deep level, thinking is a decidedly *analogue* process. Before capturing the world in concepts, thinking is *emotionally gripped*, even *affected* by the world. The *affective* is essential to human thinking. *The first thought image is goosebumps.* Artificial intelligence is incapable of thinking, for the very reason that it cannot get goosebumps. It lacks the affective-analogue dimension, the capacity to be *emotionally affected*, which lies beyond the reach of data and information.

Thinking sets out from a *totality* that precedes concepts, ideas and information. It moves in a *'field* of experience' before it turns towards the individual objects and facts in that field.[1] Being in its totality, which is the concern of thinking, is disclosed first of all in an *affective* medium, a mood: *'The mood has already disclosed, in every case, Being-in-the-world as a whole, and makes it possible first of all to direct*

37

oneself towards something.[2] Before thinking turns towards something particular, it already finds itself in a fundamental attunement. This *state-of-mind* [*Befindlichkeit*] is a distinguishing feature of human thinking. A mood is not a subjective state that rubs off on the objective world. It *is* the world. The world disclosed in a fundamental attunement is subsequently articulated by thinking in terms of concepts. Being gripped precedes comprehension, the work on the formation of concepts: 'We determined philosophizing as comprehensive questioning arising out of Dasein's being gripped in its essence. Such being gripped however is possible only from out of and within a fundamental attunement of Dasein.'[3] Humans think only because of this fundamental attunement: 'All essential thinking demands that its thoughts and utterances be newly extracted each time, like an ore, out of the basic disposition.'[4]

The human being, as 'Dasein', is always already thrown into a specific world [*bestimmte Welt*]. The world as a totality is pre-reflexively disclosed to humans. Dasein, as being-*attuned*, precedes being-*aware*. In its initial being gripped, thinking is so to speak *outside of itself*. The fundamental attunement sets it into an *outside*. Artificial intelligence does not think because it is never *outside of itself*. The German word for *spirit*, Geist, originally means *being-outside-of-oneself* or *being gripped*. Artificial intelligence may *compute* very quickly, but it lacks *spirit*. For a computer, to be gripped would only be a disturbance.

An 'analogue' is something that corresponds to another thing. As an analogue process, thinking *corresponds* to a *voice* that at-*tunes* [*be-stimmt*] it and *at-tunes* it through and through [*durch-stimmt*]. Thinking is not addressed by this being or that being but by being in its totality, the *being of beings*. Heidegger's phenomenology of attunement can be used to illustrate the fundamental difference between human thinking and artificial intelligence. In *What Is Philosophy?* Heidegger says:

> The correspondence listens to the voice of the appeal. What appeals to us as the voice of Being evokes [*be-stimmt*] our correspondence. 'Correspondence' then means: being de-termined [*be-stimmt*], *être disposé* by that which comes from the Being of being. Correspondence is necessarily and is always attuned, and not just accidentally and occasionally. It is in an attunement. And only on the basis of the attunement (disposition) does the language of correspondence obtain its precision, its tuning [*Be-stimmtheit*].[5]

Thinking *hears*, even *listens*, *eavesdrops*. Artificial intelligence is deaf. It does not hear that voice.

According to Heidegger, the 'beginning of an actual living philosophizing' is the 'awakening of a fundamental attunement', an 'attunement that pervades *us* fundamentally'.[6] The fundamental attunement is the gravity that gathers words and concepts around it. Without fundamental attunement, thinking lacks an *ordering frame*: 'If the basic disposition is lacking, then everything is a forced clatter of concepts and of the mere shells of words.'[7] The affective totality that is given with a fundamental attunement is the *analogue* dimension of thinking that cannot be represented by artificial intelligence.

According to Heidegger, the history of philosophy is the history of fundamental attunement. Descartes's thinking, for instance, is at-*tuned* [be*stimmt*] by doubt, while Plato's thinking is at-*tuned* through and through by wonder. Descartes's *cogito* is based on the fundamental attunement of doubt. Heidegger paints the following *picture of the attunement* of modern philosophy:

> For him doubt becomes that tuning in which the attunement [structure of determination] vibrates to the *ens certum*, i.e. being in certainty. *Certitudo* becomes a fixing of the *ens qua ens* which results from the unquestionability of the *cogito (ergo) sum* for man's ego. . . . The tuning of confidence to the absolute certainty of knowledge which is attainable at all times remains the *pathos* and thus the *arché* of modern philosophy.[8]

Pathos is the beginning of thinking. Artificial intelligence is *apathetic*, that is, without *pathos*, without *passion*. It *computes*.

Artificial intelligence has no access to *horizons* that are *divined* rather than clearly delineated. This 'divination' [*Ahnung*], however, is not 'the outer court before the gates of knowledge'. Rather, this divination discloses the 'great hall in which everything that can be known is kept, concealed'.[9] Heidegger locates divination in the heart. Artificial intelligence is without heart. Heartfelt thinking measures and feels *spaces* before it works on concepts. In this, it differs from computing, which does not need *spaces*: 'If this "hearty" knowing is an intimating [*Ahnen*], then we must never regard such intimating as an opining that floats around in unclarity. It has its own lucidity and decisiveness and yet remains fundamentally different from the self-assuredness of calculative understanding.'[10]

From a Heideggerian perspective, artificial intelligence is incapable of thinking because it cannot access the *totality* that is thinking's point of departure. Artificial intelligence is *worldless*. The totality, as a *semantic horizon*, comprises more than the goals that guide artificial intelligence. Thinking's way of proceeding is altogether different from that of artificial intelligence. Totality forms thinking's initial *frame*, out of which facts are created. A change in the attunement, a changing of this frame, resembles a paradigm shift that creates new facts.[11] Artificial intelligence, by contrast, processes *pre-given*, *unchanging* facts. It cannot provide new facts to be processed.

Big data creates the illusion of absolute knowledge. Things give away their secret correlations. Everything becomes computable and controllable. A new era of knowledge is proclaimed. In reality, what we have here is a pretty primitive form of knowledge. Data mining reveals correlations. According to Hegel's *Science of Logic*, correlation is the lowest form of knowledge. A correlation between A and B means that A often happens in combination with B, but we do not know *why* that is the case. It *simply is the case*. Correlations reveal a probability, not a necessity. They differ from causal relations that establish a necessity: *A causes B*. Reciprocity represents the next level of knowledge. Reciprocity means that A and B cause each other. This establishes a necessary connection between A and B, yet at this level there is still no *conceptual understanding*: 'If one does not move beyond considering a given content merely from the viewpoint of reciprocity, this is in fact an utterly conceptless way of behaving.'[12]

Only with a 'concept' [*Begriff*] can the connection between A and B be captured. The concept is the C that in-cludes [*ein-begreift*] A and B. With the help of C, the connection between A and B is *understood* [*begriffen*]. The concept forms the *frame*, the *totality*, that comprises A and B and clarifies their relation. A and B are only 'moments of a third, higher [dimension]'.[13] *Knowledge* in the proper sense of the word is possible only at the level of the concept: 'The concept is something that dwells within the things themselves, by means of which they are what they are, and to comprehend [*begreifen*] an object means accordingly to become conscious of its concept [*Begriff*].'[14] Only by way of the comprehensive *concept* C can the connection between A and B fully be understood. Reality itself is transformed into knowledge by being captured by the concept.

Big data provides a rudimentary knowledge. It remains limited to correlations and pattern recognition, in which, however, nothing is *understood*. A concept forms a totality that en-*closes* and in-*cludes* its moments. Totality is a form of conclusion [*Schluß*]. A concept is a conclusion: 'Everything is a syllogism [*Schluß*]' means 'everything is a *concept*'.[15] Reason is also a conclusion: '*everything rational* [*alles Vernünftige*] *is a syllogism*'.[16] Big data is *additive*. What is additive does not form a totality, a conclusion. It lacks a concept, that is, the grip that in*cludes* the parts in a totality. Artificial intelligence never reaches the conceptual level of knowledge. It does not *understand* [*begreift*] the results it computes. Computing differs from thinking insofar as computing does not form concepts and does not proceed from one conclusion to the next.

Artificial intelligence learns from the past. The future it computes is not a future in the proper sense. It is *event-blind*. Thinking, however, has the character of an event.

It puts something *altogether other* into the world. Artificial intelligence lacks precisely the *negativity of rupture* that allows something genuinely *new* to begin. Artificial intelligence ultimately continues the *same*. Intelligence means *choosing between* (*inter-legere*). All it does is make a choice between options that are *given in advance*, ultimately between 'one' and 'zero'. It does not move, beyond what is given, to *untrodden paths*.

Genuine thinking brings forth a *new world*. It is on the way towards the *altogether other*, towards *somewhere else*: 'The word of thinking is not picturesque; it is without charm. . . . Just the same, thinking changes the world. It changes it in the ever darker depths of a riddle, depths which as they grow darker offer promise of a greater brightness.'[17] Machine intelligence does not advance to this darker depth of a riddle. Information and data have no *depth*. Human thinking is more than computing and problem solving. It *brightens* and *clears* the world. It brings forth an *altogether other world*. The main danger that arises from machine intelligence is that human thinking will adapt to it and *itself* become *mechanical*.

Thinking is nourished by Eros. In Plato, Logos and Eros enter into an intimate relation. Eros is the condition for the possibility of thinking. Heidegger follows Plato on this point. On the way towards unknown territory, thinking is given wings by Eros: 'I call it Eros, the oldest of the gods according to Parmenides. . . . The beat of that god's wings moves me each time I take a substantial step in my thinking and venture onto untrodden paths.'[18] Computing is without Eros. Data and information do not *seduce*.

According to Deleuze, philosophy begins with a *faire l'idiot* – with 'making oneself an idiot'.[19] Thinking is

43

characterized not by intelligence but by idiocy. Every philosopher who creates a new idiom, a new thinking, a new language, is an idiot. The philosopher bids farewell to all that *went before*. A philosopher inhabits a *virgin, hitherto undescribed immanent level* of thinking. By adopting the principle of *faire l'idiot*, thinking risks the leap into the altogether other, ventures on untrodden paths. The history of philosophy is a history of idiocy, of idiotic leaps: 'The old idiot wanted indubitable truths at which he could arrive by himself: in the meantime he would doubt everything . . . The new idiot has no wish for indubitable truths . . . and wills the absurd – this is not the same image of thought.'[20] Artificial intelligence cannot think because it is incapable of *faire l'idiot. It is too intelligent for becoming an idiot.*

Views of Things

Quelle étonnante servilité! Les choses sont sages comme des images. A la lettre: comme des images! Elles n'inquiètent plus du tout les hommes. Aussi, même du coin de l'oeil, ne les considerènt-ils plus.

[What an astounding submissiveness! The things are tame, like pictures. Literally like pictures! They no longer worry people at all. *And thus they are no longer noticed by them, not even out of the corners of their eyes.*[1]]

D'abord la chose est l'autre, le tout autre qui dicte ou qui écrit la loi, . . . une injonction infiniment, insatiablement impérieuse à laquelle je dois m'assujettir.

[Beforehand, the thing is the other, the entirely other which dictates or which writes the law, . . . an infinitely, insatiably imperious injunction to which I ought to subject myself.][2]

The Villainy of Things

In the *Mickey Mouse* cartoons, representations of material reality change over time.[3] In the earlier episodes, things behave treacherously. They take on a life of their own, even a waywardness. They are unpredictable actors. The hero is constantly grappling with them. He is literally thrown around by them, and they take pleasure in tormenting him. It is not at all safe for him to be near them. Doors, chairs, folding beds or vehicles can at any time turn into dangerous objects and traps. Mechanical things are diabolical. There are constant crashes. The hero is exposed to the vagaries of things. They are a permanent source of frustration. The cartoons are entertaining to a large extent because of the *villainy of things*.

In his early films, Charlie Chaplin is also hopelessly at the mercy of the villainy of things. They fly around him, and they block his way. His battles with things create the films' slapstick humour. Torn out of their functional context, the things lead lives of their own. The films present an anarchy of things. In *The Pawnshop*, for instance, Chaplin, the pawnshop owner, examines an alarm clock with a stethoscope and a hammer, as if it were a body, and opens it with a manual drill and a can opener. The mechanical parts of the disassembled alarm clock then begin to move around as if they were alive.[4]

The villainy of things is now probably a thing of the past. We are no longer maltreated by things. They are not destructive; they do not offer any resistance. The sting has been taken out of them. We do not perceive them in their otherness or as alien. This weakens our *feeling for reality*. In particular, digitalization intensifies the de-realization of the world because it de-reifies it. Derrida's remark about the thing as the 'entirely other' (*le tout autre*), as dictating a 'law' to us to which we need to subject ourselves, now sounds strange. Things are submissive. They are submitted to our needs.

Today, even Mickey Mouse leads a digital, smart and immaterial life. His world is digitalized and informationalized. In the new series *Mickey Mouse Clubhouse*, the representation of material reality is markedly different from that in the early episodes. Things no longer have an independent life; they are obedient tools for solving problems. Life itself is seen as problem solving. The handling of things no longer involves conflict. Things no longer appear as unruly actors.

For example, when Mickey and his friends end up in a trap, they need only to shout 'Oh, Tootles' and the 'Handy Dandy machine' appears. The screen of the machine, which looks like a round smartphone, displays a menu of four 'Mouseketools', that is, four objects from which they can choose in order to solve the problem. The Handy Dandy machine has a ready solution for every problem. The hero no longer collides with physical reality. He does not have to deal with the resistance of things. In this way, children are fed the idea that there is nothing that cannot be done, that there is a quick solution, an app, for everything and that life itself is nothing but a series of problems to be solved.

The Reverse of Things

Sinbad is shipwrecked. He and his comrades find themselves on a small island that, to Sinbad, looks like the garden of paradise. They stroll around and hunt. When they light a fire to cook their kill, the ground suddenly warps. Trees collapse. The island is, in fact, the back of a giant fish, which has been resting for so long that fertile soil has formed on its back. The heat of the fire has disturbed the fish. It dives down into the deep sea, and Sinbad and his comrades are thrown into the water. In Ernst Bloch's reading of the fairy tale, it becomes an allegory for our relationship with things. Bloch objects to the instrumental treatment of things. He sees human culture as a very fragile institution built on the 'reverse of things': 'We know only the front or right side of their technical subservience, their benign incorporation', but we see neither their 'underside' nor 'what it all floats in'.[5]

Bloch considers the possibility that the subservience of things is only their front, the part of them that is turned towards us, and that they actually 'belong to another world, one only interspersed into this one'.[6] He suspects that, behind their subservience, things lead an irrational life of their own that runs counter to human intentions:

The fire in the stove burns even when we're not around. Therefore, we say, it must have been burning in the meantime, since the room is now warm. Yet that is not certain, and what the fire was doing before, what the furniture was doing during our absence, is obscure. No proposition about it can be proven, and none, even the most fantastical, can be refuted. Precisely: the mice dance on the table, and what did the table do – what was it – in the meantime? That on our return everything stands as it was, 'as though nothing had happened', can

48

be the most uncanny thing of all. . . . . For many it is an uncanny feeling from early on, seeing things only when we see them.[7]

Maybe the Internet of Things is a response to our deep-seated fear that things could be up to no good in our absence. The infosphere puts things in chains. The Internet of Things is their prison. It tames things and turns them into servants catering to our needs.

In the past, humans apparently granted things more independence. In a very popular novel by the philosopher Friedrich Theodor Vischer, *Auch Einer* (1879), things get into a lot of mischief. The protagonist constantly feels threatened by the 'villainy of the object'. The things have really got to him. He is at war with them. Occasionally, he takes revenge by executing them:

> From dawn till late at night, as long as some human being is around, objects think about mischief, about villainy. One needs to treat them the way a tamer treats a wild beast after daring to enter its cage: he fixes his eyes on its eyes, and the beast fixes its eyes on his . . . Thus, every object lies in wait – pencil, quill, inkpot, paper, cigar, glass, lamp – always, always waiting for the moment one is distracted. . . . And just as the tiger leaps at his hapless victim the very moment he feels unobserved, so does the cursed object.[8]

In the literature of the past, things often appear as subjects with wills of their own. Stories like Joseph Addison's *Adventures of a Shilling* (1710) or James Fenimore Cooper's *Autobiography of a Pocket-Handkerchief* (1843), in which things are the protagonists, telling the stories of their own lives, would be unthinkable today. In the twentieth century, too, many works of literature involved people confronting the idiosyncratic lives of things. These cases show that there were still cracks in the project of modernity: the project of instrumentalizing things and making them totally available. Perception was still open to the *underside and the reverse of things*.

The protagonist of Robert Musil's *The Confusions of Young Törless*, for instance, possesses the 'mysterious quality' of being 'attacked by inanimate things, mere objects, as well, sometimes as if by a hundred silent, questioning eyes'. Things *look at* him. Nondescript things appear to him as if they could speak. The world is full of 'soundless voices'.[9] In those days, the *other as gaze*, the *other as voice*, was present. Sartre was also still familiar with what it means *to be touched by things*. The protagonist of *Nausea* frequently comes *into contact* with things, an experience that fills him with terror:

> Objects should not touch because they are not alive. You use them, put them back in place, you live among them: they are useful, nothing more. But they touch me, it is unbearable. I am afraid of being in contact with them as though they were living beasts.[10]

In Sartre's world, the *other* still has integrity. The *other as gaze* is constitutive of the relation to the world. Even the 'rustling of branches', or 'the slight opening of a shutter, or a light movement of a curtain', is perceived as a gaze.[11] Today, the world is gaze-less. It no longer looks at us. The world has lost its *otherness*.

For Rilke, things emanate warmth. He dreams of lying with things:

I want to sleep one time beside each thing, grow drowsy from its warmth, on its breathing dream up and down, sense in all my limbs its dear relaxed naked being-near and become strong through the scent of its sleep and then in the morning, early, before it wakes, ahead of all farewells, pass on, pass on.[12]

Beautiful crafted things warm the heart. The *warmth of the hands* is passed on to the things. Mechanical coldness does away with the warmth of things. In modernity, things cool down and become intractable objects. Walter Benjamin also notes this cooling down of things:

Warmth is ebbing from things. The objects of daily use gently but insistently repel us. Day by day, in overcoming the sum of secret resistances – not only the overt ones – that they put in our way, we have an immense labour to perform. We must compensate for their coldness with our warmth if they are not to freeze us to death, and handle their spines with infinite dexterity, if we are not to perish by bleeding.[13]

It has been some time since things had 'spines'. Digitalization has deprived things of any 'defiant' materiality, any intractability. They have entirely lost the character of *obicere*. They offer us no resistance. Informatons do not have spines that must be handled with infinite dexterity. Rather, they closely follow the contours of our needs. No one gets hurt handling a smooth smartphone.

51

These days, things are not even cooled down. They have neither cold nor warmth; they are worn out. All their vitality is waning. They no longer represent a counterpart to humans. They are not *opposing bodies*. Who, today, feels looked at, or spoken to, by things? Who perceives the countenances of things? Who detects a living physiognomy in things? To whom do things appear to have a soul? Who suspects that things have lives of their own? Who feels threatened or enchanted by things? Who feels happy at the warm sight of things? Who looks on in astonishment at their alienness? Do today's children still tiptoe around dimly lit rooms, their hearts pounding, while tables, wardrobes and curtains pull wild faces at them?

Today's world is very poor in *gaze* and *voice*. It neither looks at nor speaks to us. The world has lost its *otherness*. The digital screen determines our experience of the world and shields us from reality. The world is de-realized, de-reified and disembodied. The emboldened ego is no longer touched by the other. On the *reverse of things*, it sees only a reflection of itself. The *disappearance of the other* is actually a dramatic event. But it happens so gradually as to be imperceptible. The other as a secret, as a gaze, as a voice, disappears. The other, deprived of otherness, is reduced to an available, consumable object.

The disappearance of the other also takes hold of the world of things. Things lose their gravity, their independent life and their waywardness.

We cannot enter into a *relation* with a world that consists exclusively of available, consumable objects. It is also impossible to be in a *relation* with information. A relation requires an independent *counterpart*, *mutuality*, a *Thou*: 'When *Thou* is spoken, the speaker has no thing; he has indeed nothing. But he takes his stand in relation.'[14] An available, consumable object is not a Thou but an It. The absent relation and attachment creates a significant poverty in world. The plethora of digital objects in particular leads to a loss of world. A screen is very poor in world and reality. Without any counterpart, without any *Thou*, we are caught up in ourselves. Depression is nothing other than a pathologically intensified poverty in world. Digitalization is partly responsible for the spread of depression. Infospheres intensify our self-referentiality. We submit everything to our needs. Only a *revitalization of the other* could free us of our poverty in world.

Ghosts

In Kafka's 'The Cares of a Family Man', a recalcitrant thing named Odradek haunts the house. It worries the family man. Odradek is a 'star-shaped spool for a thread' that can move independently on two stick-like protrusions as if on legs.[15] Odradek is not subservient or submissive. It is a thing, but it does not appear to have any kind of function. Nothing about it points to functionality:

> One is tempted to believe that the creature once had some sort of intelligible shape and is now only a broken-down remnant. Yet this does not seem to be the case; at least there is no sign of it; nowhere is there an unfinished or unbroken surface to suggest anything of the kind; the whole thing looks senseless enough, but in its own way perfectly finished. In any case, closer scrutiny

is impossible, since Odradek is extraordinary nimble and can never be laid hold of.[16]

Odradek is also unlocatable. It has 'no fixed abode'.[17] It spends most of its time in *interstitial spaces*, such as the staircase or corridor. Sometimes it is not seen for months on end. It embodies the *other*, the *wholly other*. It follows its *own law*.

Odradek may be very strong-willed but, as the narrator says in the conclusion, he 'does no harm to anyone that one can see'.[18] Kafka thought very differently about non-things. In a letter to Milena, he writes that all his misfortune derives from writing letters.[19] Letters 'must have brought wrack and ruin to the souls of the world'. Writing letters 'is actually an intercourse with ghosts'. One can think of someone who is far away, or hold someone close, but all else is 'beyond human power'. Written kisses do not reach their destination. Along the way, they are intercepted by ghosts, who drink them up. 'People sense this and struggle against it.' Thus, mankind invents the railway, the car and the aeroplane 'in order to eliminate as much of the ghosts' power as possible and to attain . . . a tranquillity of soul'. But all this is to no avail; these are nothing but 'inventions devised at the moment of crashing'. The opponent is so much stronger: 'after the postal system, the ghosts invented the telegraph, the telephone, the wireless'. The ghosts will not starve, but mankind, Kafka concludes, 'will perish'.

In the face of digitalization, Kafka would be resigned. He would observe that, by inventing the internet, email and the smartphone, the ghosts had won their final victory over mankind. Networks buzz with ghosts. Infospheres are indeed ghostly spaces. In an infosphere, nothing is *arrestable* [*dingfest*]. Non-things are perhaps the food of the ghosts.

Digital communication severely impairs human relations. Today, even if we are not *related* to one another, we are connected wherever we are. Digital communication is extensive. It lacks intensity. Being connected is not the same as being in a *relation*. Everywhere, *Thou* is replaced by *It*. Digital communication abolishes the personal counterpart, the *countenance*, the *gaze*, *physical presence*. It thus accelerates the *disappearance of the other*. The *hell of the same* is inhabited by ghosts.

Humans are intimate beings [*Nahwesen*]. Intimacy, however, is not the same as a lack of distance. Distance is part of it. Nearness and distance belong together. The human being is thus simultaneously a being of nearness and a being of distance. This is why Kafka says that we can hold someone who is near or think of someone who is far away but all else is beyond our power. Because it makes everything *gapless*, digital communication destroys both nearness and distance. The *relation to the other* requires distance. Distance ensures that the Thou is not reduced to It. In the age of *gaplessness*, relation gives way to *contact without distance*.

Informatons completely lack the idiosyncrasy of things. They are in every respect opposed to Odradek, the recalcitrant thing. The nature of informatons is completely exhausted by their functionality. They submit themselves to orders. The informaton named Alexa – which, in contrast to Odradek, has a fixed abode – is very talkative. As opposed to the mute Odradek – someone to whom, according to Kafka, 'you put no difficult questions'[20]

– Alexa responds to every question, no matter how complicated it may be, and willingly provides an answer. In our *smart homes* without things, the 'family man' will have no cares.

The Magic of Things

We perceive the world primarily through information. We cannot perceive *intensities* because of the layer of information that covers and shields things, like a gapless membrane. Information *represents* reality. Its dominance makes it harder to *experience presence*.[21] We constantly consume information. Information reduces *touching*. Our perception loses depth and intensity, physicality and volume. It does not immerse itself in reality's *layer of presence*.

The sheer volume of reality-cloaking information undermines the *thing level* of reality. Hugo von Hofmannsthal already stated that 'words have placed themselves in front of the things. Hearsay has swallowed the world.'[22] In his famous Chandos letter, the fictional narrator tells of his epiphanies, his experiences of presence. Inconspicuous things, such as a 'half-filled pitcher' with a 'beetle swimming on the surface', 'a crippled apple-tree', 'a moss-covered stone',[23] or a harrow left in the fields 'over which the eye usually glides with a natural indifference', all of a sudden 'assume for [him] a character so exalted and moving' that they cause a 'silent but suddenly rising flood of divine sensation'.[24] Epiphanic experiences of intensity cause 'a kind of feverish thinking in a medium more immediate, more liquid, more glowing than words'.[25] The text invokes a *magic* relationship with the world that is not characterized by *representation* (that is, by ideas or meaning) but by immediate *touching* and *presence*.

The experience of presence is brought about neither by the 'vision of the starry sky' nor by the 'majestic booming of an organ'.[26] Rather, the source of wordless delight is a 'combination of trifles'.[27] In such epiphanic moments, the human being enters 'into a new and hopeful relationship with the whole of existence' and 'begins to think with the heart'.[28] The epiphany includes moments of deep 'peace'.[29] The narrator longs for a *thing language* 'in which mute things speak to me and wherein I may one day have to justify myself before an unknown judge'.[30]

When one pays more attention to things, one forgets oneself, loses oneself. When the ego gets *weak*, it is able to hear that mute thing language. The *experience of presence* requires *exposure, vulnerability*. Without a *wound*, I ultimately hear only the echo of myself. A *wound* is an opening, an *ear for the other*. Epiphanic moments are no longer possible today because the ego is becoming stronger and stronger. The ego is not *touched* by things.

Barthes's theory of photography can be applied to reality itself. He distinguishes between two elements of photography. The first element, the *studium*, concerns the wide field of information that we *register* when looking at a photograph. It is the 'field of unconcerned desire, of various interest, of inconsequential taste: *I like / I don't like*. The *studium* is of the order of *liking*, not of *loving*.' It is accompanied by no more than 'vague, slippery, irresponsible interest'.[31] Visual information is perfectly capable of being shocking, but it does not 'injure'. It does not cause 'consternation'. The *studium* is completely devoid of *severity*. It does not create *intensities*. It is based on a form of perception that is extensive, additive and cumulative. The *studium* is a *reading* of a photograph. It lacks all magic.

The second element of photography is called *punctum*. It interrupts the *studium*. Something 'shoots out of [the scene] like an arrow, and pierces me'.[32] The *punctum* punctuates the continuum of information. It is a place of the highest intensity and concentration. *Something indefinable* inheres in it, something beyond all representation: 'The incapacity to name is a good symptom for disturbance. . . . The effect is certain but unlocatable, it does not find its sign, its name; it is sharp and yet lands in a vague zone of myself.'[33]

The *studium* is invested with a 'sovereign consciousness'.[34] I let my sovereign attention glide across the vast field of information. The *punctum*, by contrast, puts me into a condition of radical passivity. It makes me weak. I suffer a loss of self. Without any conscious decision on my part, something 'is poignant to me'. Something 'pricks me' and 'bruises me'.[35] I am touched and moved by something *singular*. Something *nameless* breaks into an unknown zone within myself, a zone that is outside of my control.

Barthes calls photographs that are wholly *studium* 'unary'.[36] They simply convey plausible information. When it is so diluted as to become consumable information, reality itself becomes unary. Reality as information belongs to the order of *to like*, not that of *to love*. *Like* swamps the world. Inherent in every intense experience is the *negativity of the other*. The positivity of *like* transforms the world into the *hell of the same*.

For Barthes, pornographic photographs fall into the category of unary photography. Whereas erotic photography produces 'disturbed, fissured' photos, pornographic photographs are smooth.[37] Information never reveals *ruptures*: there is no *erotic information*. The nature of information is pornographic. What is fully *presented* and completely *exhibited* does not seduce. Eroticism requires a 'blind field', something that escapes visibility and the obviousness of information: 'The presence (the dynamics) of this blind field is, I believe, what distinguishes the erotic photograph from the pornographic photograph.'[38] The 'blind field' is the *place of the imagination*. It opens up only once the *eyes are closed*.

The *punctum of reality* penetrates the field of representation and allows *presence* to burst in. It creates epiphanic moments. Digitalization totalizes the *studium* by reducing reality to information. Nothing shoots out of the digital screen like an arrow to pierce the observer. Information does not have *arrow tips*. It bounces off the strengthened ego. The mass of information that cloaks reality shields the *punctum of reality* from perception. The noise of information prevents the experience of a presence, even *revelation*, that might house a *moment of silence*.

Freud calls a perceptual complex that eludes representation a 'thing'. A thing 'makes an impression' because no attributes can be assigned to it.[39] This impressive singularity, the *negativity of the wholly other*, is characteristic of the thing. It thus marks a *rupture* within the symbolic order, that is, within the *studium*. Lacan says of the thing: 'What one finds in *das Ding* is the true secret.'[40] The thing as a *blind spot* is the opposite of information and transparency. It is the *opaque* par excellence. It signifies something that stubbornly retreats into an *underground*. While the normal things of everyday perception are representatives of the symbolic order, the secret *thing-in-itself* is a NON-THING (*achose*).[41] The NON-THING is the *real* that escapes the *symbolic*. The NON-THING slips through the net of representation. It is the *punctum of reality*, that 'blind field' (*champ aveugle*) or 'subtle beyond' (*hors-champ subtil*) that undermines the studium, the vast field of information.[42]

The Forgetfulness of Things in Art

Artworks are things. Even linguistic works of art, such as poems, which we normally do not treat like things, have the character of a thing. Rilke, in a letter to Lou Andreas-Salomé, writes: 'Somehow I too must manage to make things; written, not plastic things, – realities that proceed from handwork.'[43] A poem – a form made of *signifiers*, linguistic signs – is a thing because it cannot be dissolved into meanings. We can read a poem for its meaning, but the poem is not exhausted by its meaning. A poem has a sensual-physical dimension that eludes its sense, the *signified*. It is the *excess of the signifier* that condenses [*verdichtet*] the poem [*das Gedicht*] into a thing.

We cannot read a thing. A poem, as a thing, resists the kind of reading that consumes sense and emotion, as in the case of crime stories or cheap novels. Such reading is looking for something to be uncovered. It is pornographic. A poem, by contrast, resists providing any kind of 'novelistic satisfaction', any kind of consumption.[44] Pornographic reading is opposed to an *erotic reading* that *lingers* with the text as a body, as a thing. Poems don't sit well with our pornographic and consumerist age. This, in particular, is the reason that we rarely read poems any more.

Robert Walser describes the poem as a beautiful body, as a physical thing:

A beautiful poem, in my opinion, has to be a beautiful body that blossoms forth from . . . words that are unmindfully, almost without following an idea, put on paper. These words are the skin that stretches tightly over the content, that is, the body. The art is not to say words but to form a poem body, that is, to ensure that the words are only the means by which a poem body is formed.[45]

The words are put on paper 'without following an idea' and 'unmindfully': the poet is freed from the intention of giving the words an unambiguous meaning. The poet abandons himself to an almost unconscious process. The poem is woven of signifiers that are freed from the drudgery of having to produce meaning. The poet is *not following an idea*. He is characterized by a mimetic naivety. His concern is to form a body, a thing, out of words. The words are the skin, and the skin does not enclose a meaning. It stretches tightly over the body. Writing poetry is an *act of love*, an *erotic play with the body*.

Walser's *materialism* consists in his understanding of the poem as a body. Poetry is not the work of forming meaning but that of forming bodies. Signifiers do not primarily refer to the signified; rather, passing the signified by, they condense into a beautiful, mysterious, *seductive* body. Reading is not a hermeneutic but a haptic act, a touch, a caress. Reading snuggles up to the *skin of the poem*. It *enjoys the poem's body*. The poem, as a body, makes us feel a special *presence* beyond the realm of *representation*, the realm to which hermeneutics is dedicated.

Art is increasingly moving away from the materialist view of the work of art as a thing. Because it is not committed to meaning, this materialism allows for the free and easy play of signifiers. It views language as material to be played with. Francis Ponge would wholeheartedly endorse Walser's materialism: 'From the very moment that words (and verbal expressions) are seen as material, it is very agreeable to occupy yourself with them. Just as it can be agreeable for a painter to be occupied with colours and forms. Very enjoyable to play with them.'[46] Language is a playground, an 'amusement park'. Words are not primarily the bearers of meaning. Rather, the point is 'to gain as much pleasure as possible from them beyond their meaning'.[47] Accordingly, an art that is committed to meaning is *hostile to pleasure*.

Ponge's poetics aims to express the otherness, the idiosyncrasy, of things, independent of their utility. In this context, the function of language is not to signify things, that is, to *represent* them. Rather, Ponge's thing perspective *reifies* [*verdinglicht*] the words, bringing their status close to that of a thing. In its mimetic naivety, this poetics pictures the *secret correspondence between language and thing*. As in the case of Walser, the poet does *not follow an idea* at all.

The voice also has a thing-like, bodily dimension, which reveals itself especially in its 'grain', in the 'voluptuousness of its sounds-signifiers'.[48] The thing-like aspect of the voice makes the tongue and the membranes, their desire, audible. It forms the *sensual skin of the voice*. The voice is not only articulated but *given a body*. The voice that is fully exhausted by meaning is without body, without enjoyment, without desire. Like Walser, Barthes explicitly speaks of the *skin*, the *body* of language:

> something is there, manifest and idiosyncratic (one hears only that), beyond (or before) the meaning of the words . . . something which is directly the cantor's body, brought to your ears in one and the same movement from deep down in the cavities, the muscles, the membranes, the cartilages . . . as though a single skin lined the inner flesh of the performer and the music he sings.[49]

Barthes distinguishes between two kinds of singing. 'Geno-song' is ruled by the pleasure principle, the body, desire; 'pheno-song' is dedicated to communication, the transmission of meaning.[50] In pheno-song, consonants, working on sense and meaning, are dominant. Geno-song, by contrast, uses consonants only as a 'springboard for the admirable vowels'.[51] Vowels house the voluptuous body, desire. They form the *skin* of language. They cause goosebumps. Pheno-song, made up of consonants, by contrast, does not *touch* us.

A work of art, being a thing, is not just a bearer of meaning. It does not *illustrate* anything. The process of expression is directed not by a clear concept but by an indeterminate fever, a delirium, an intensity, an urge or desire that cannot be articulated. In his essay 'Cezanne's Doubt', Maurice Merleau-Ponty writes:

> What he expresses cannot, therefore, be the translation of a clearly defined thought, since such clear thoughts are those that have already been said within ourselves

or by others. 'Conception' cannot precede 'execution'. Before expression, there is nothing but an indeterminate fever.[52]

A work of art *signifies* [*bedeutet*] more than all the meanings [*Bedeutungen*] that could be taken from it. This excess meaning, paradoxically, is owed to a renunciation of meaning. It derives from the *excess of the signifier* [*Signifikanten*].

What is problematic about today's art is its inclination to communicate a preconceived opinion, a moral or political conviction: that is, its inclination to communicate information.[53] Conception precedes execution. As a result, art degenerates into illustration. The expressive process is no longer determined by an indeterminate fever. Art is no longer *handwork* that forms matter, *without intention*, into a thing, but thought work that communicates a prefabricated idea. Art is seized by a *forgetfulness of things*. Art allows itself to be put in the service of communication. It becomes *lopsided*; it leans *towards information and discourse*. It wants to *instruct* rather than *seduce*.

Information destroys the *stillness* of the work of art: 'Original paintings are still and silent in a sense that information never is.'[54] When we look at an image with only information in mind, we miss its idiosyncrasy, its magic. It is the *excess of the signifier* that accounts for the *magic* and *mystery* of a work of art. The secret of a work of art does not consist in the fact that it hides information that could be unveiled. What is mysterious, rather, is the fact that signifiers circulate without being stopped in their tracks by a signified:

The secret.

The seductive, initiatory quality of that which cannot be said because it makes no sense, and of that which is not said even though it gets around. . . . The complicity has nothing to do with some hidden piece of information. Besides, even if we wanted to reveal the secret we could not, since there is nothing to say. Everything that can be revealed lies outside the secret. . . . It is the opposite of communication, and yet it can be shared.[55]

Secrets do not sit well with the regime of information and communication. Secrets are the opponents of information. They are language *murmuring*, without, however, saying anything. Essential to art is a 'seduction beneath discourse, an invisible seduction, moving from sign to sign – a secret circulation'.[56] Seduction takes place below meaning, outside of hermeneutics. Seduction is *faster* and *more nimble* than sense and meaning.

The work of art has two aspects, one that is turned towards representation and one that is turning away from it. We may call them the *pheno-layer* and the *geno-layer* respectively. Art that is leaning towards discourse, art that moralizes and politicizes, has no *geno-layer*. It has opinions but no *desire*. The geno-layer, the place of the secret, resists the assignment of meaning, and so lends the work of art the aura of the NON-THING. The NON-THING *impresses* because it does not inform. It is the *reverse*, the mysterious backyard, the 'subtle *beyond*' (*hors-champ subtil*) of the artwork, even its *unconscious*. It resists the disenchantment of art.

Heidegger is strongly dedicated to work and to the hand, as if he sensed that the human being of the future would be handless and inclined to play rather than work. One of his lectures on Aristotle begins thus: 'Aristotle was born, worked, and died.'[57] Thinking is work. Later, Heidegger called thinking handwork: 'Perhaps thinking, too, is just something like building a cabinet [*Schrein*]. At any rate, it is handwork.'[58] The hand makes thinking a decidedly analogue process. Heidegger would say: artificial intelligence does not think because it does not have a hand.

Heidegger's *hand* is determined to defend the terrestrial order against the digital order. Digital is derived from *digitus*, meaning finger. With our fingers, we *count* and *calculate*. They are numerical, that is, digital. Heidegger explicitly distinguishes between the hand and the fingers. The typewriter, requiring only the use of the fingertips, 'withdraws from man the essential rank of the hand'.[59] The typewriter destroys the 'word' by degrading it; the word becomes 'a means of communication', that is, information.[60] The typewritten word 'no longer comes and goes by means of the writing hand, the properly acting hand'.[61] Only 'handwriting' approaches the essential realm of the word.[62] The typewriter, Heidegger says, is a 'signless cloud [*Wolke*]',[63] that is, a numerical cloud [*Wolke*], a *Cloud* that conceals the essence of the word. The hand is a 'sign' because it points towards what 'awards [*zusprechen*] itself to language'. Only the hand receives the gift of thinking. For Heidegger, the typewriter is the precursor of the computer. It turns the 'word' into 'information'. The typewriter foreshadows the digital. The construction of the computer is made possible by the 'process in which language increasingly becomes merely an instrument of *information*'.[64] The hand does not count or compute. It represents the non-countable, the non-calculable, the 'singular as such, which, as one in its singleness, is uniquely the uniquely unifying One that precedes all number'.[65]

Heidegger's analysis of equipment in *Being and Time* shows that the hand is what discloses to us the environment in its original form. A thing appears initially as something available to our hands, as 'ready-to-hand'. When I reach for a pen, it does not appear to me as an object with certain qualities. If I want to imagine the pen as an object, I have to draw my hand back and purposefully stare at the pen. The grasping hand experiences the thing at a more primordial level than the representing intuition:

> the less we just stare at the hammer-Thing, and the more we seize hold of it and use it, the more primordial does our relationship to it become, and the more unveiledly is it encountered as that which it is – as equipment. The hammering itself uncovers the specific 'manipulability' [*Handlichkeit*] of the hammer. The kind of Being which equipment possesses – in which it manifests itself in its own right – we call '*readiness-to-hand*' [*Zuhandenheit*].[66]

The hand *anticipates* [*greift vor*] every representation. Heidegger's thinking always attempts to advance to a sphere of experience that precedes but is blocked by

67

representational and objectifying thinking. The *hand* has special access to the primordial sphere of being that precedes all forms of objectification.

In *Being and Time*, the thing, as equipment, is experienced as useful. In his second analysis of equipment in 'The Origin of the Work of Art', Heidegger tries to advance to an even deeper sphere of the thing's being, one that precedes even usefulness: 'The equipmentality of equipment consists indeed in its usefulness. But this itself rests in the fullness of an essential being of the equipment. We call this reliability.'[67] 'Reliability' is a primary experience of the thing that precedes its usefulness. Heidegger illustrates 'reliability' through the example of a painting by Vincent Van Gogh of a pair of leather shoes. Why does Heidegger choose these shoes as an example? Shoes protect the *foot*, which is in many respects akin to the *hand*. Interestingly, Heidegger explicitly draws attention to the foot, which, given that everyone knows what shoes are for, is not necessary: 'We will take as an example an everyday piece of equipment, a pair of peasant shoes. . . . Equipment of this kind serves as footwear.'[68]

The Van Gogh painting actually seems to show the artist's own shoes. They are apparently men's shoes. But Heidegger makes idiosyncratic decisions in his reading:

> The peasant woman wears her shoes in the field. Only then do they become what they are. They are all the more genuinely so the less the peasant woman thinks of her shoes while she is working, or even looks at them, or is aware of them in any way at all. This is how the shoes actually serve.[69]

This passage is reminiscent of the analysis of equipment in *Being and Time*. As soon as I take the hammer-Thing into my hand and hammer, instead of just staring at it, it appears to me for what it is, that is, as equipment. Similarly, the shoes actually serve as shoes when the peasant woman walks and stands in them. But the essence of the shoe-Thing is not usefulness. In a pictorial language, Heidegger points to a level of experience that precedes usefulness:

> From out of the dark opening of the well-worn insides of the shoes the toil of the worker's tread stares forth. In the crudely solid heaviness of the shoes accumulates the tenacity of the slow trudge through the far-stretching and ever-uniform furrows of the field swept by a raw wind. On the leather lies the dampness and richness of the soil. Under the soles slides the loneliness of the field-path as evening falls. The shoes vibrate with the silent call of the earth, its silent gift of the ripening grain, its unexplained self-refusal in the wintry field. This equipment is pervaded by uncomplaining worry as to the certainty of bread, wordless joy at having once more withstood want, trembling before the impending birth, and shivering at the surrounding menace of death. This equipment belongs *to the earth* and finds protection in the *world* of the peasant woman.[70]

The 'reliability' of things consists in the fact that they embed human beings in those relations to the world that make life stable. With its 'reliability', the thing is a world-thing. Its reliability is part of the terrestrial order. Today, the thing is decoupled from this *world-founding* wealth of relations and exhausts itself in pure functionality. Thus, it is no longer reliable:

> The individual piece of equipment becomes worn out and used up. . . . In this way equipmental being withers away, sinks to the level of mere equipment. Such dwindling of equipmental being is the disappearance of its reliability. . . . Now nothing but sheer utility remains visible.[71]

Human Dasein has its *footings* on the earth. Heidegger's foot stands for *being grounded on the soil*. It connects human beings with the earth, which gives them stability and abode. Heidegger's *country path* 'quietly escorts one's steps along the winding trail through the expanse of the sparse landscape'.[72] The thing and its reliability take care that human beings *establish a firm footing* on the earth. The foot provides another clue as to why Heidegger holds on to the hand with such determination. Hand and foot point to the *site* of Heidegger's thinking. They embody the terrestrial order. The handless humans of the future are also footless. They hover above the earth in the digital Cloud.

Heidegger's thing is a world-thing: 'The thing things world.'[73] The verb 'thinging', belonging to the thing, means 'gathering'. The thing 'gathers' the meaningful relations in which human Dasein is embedded. The world structure that founds meaning Heidegger calls the 'fourfold'. The world consists of four elements that provide meaning and stability: 'earth' and 'sky', the 'divinities' and the 'mortals'.[74] For Heidegger, things include 'brook and hill' [*Bach und Berg*], 'heron and roe' [*Reiher und Reh*], 'mirror and clasp' [*Spiegel und Spange*], 'book and picture'

[*Buch und Bild*] and 'crown and cross' [*Krone und Kreuz*].[75] The consistent *alliteration* suggests a simple world order that has to be reflected in the things. Heidegger asks us to rely on the *metre*, on the *rhythm*, of the terrestrial order – to place ourselves in the hands of the *weight of the world*.

Heidegger insists on the *intrinsic measure* of the earth. His belief is that there is an 'approval or ordering' beyond the human will, and that humans need to obey this ordering.[76] An abode is not *produced* but *approved*. The later Heidegger had in mind a *care-free Dasein*, a 'safebeing' that is, however, beyond human influence:

> Safe, *securus, sine cura* means: without care. Care has here the nature of deliberate self-assertion along the ways and by the means of absolute production. . . . The safebeing is the sheltered repose in the attraction-nexus of the whole attraction.[77]

Humans, Heidegger says, are the 'be-thinged'.[78] The 'thing' shelters the 'attraction-nexus of the whole attraction' that takes care of the stability, the 'safebeing'. Heidegger sets himself against the beginnings of the digital order, in which the world 'remains orderable as a system of information'.[79] The digital order strives for the un-thinged [*das Un-Bedingte*], whereas in the terrestrial order humans are the be-thinged:

> Man is about to hurl himself upon the entire earth and its atmosphere, to arrogate to himself the hidden working of nature in the form of energy . . . This same defiant man is incapable of saying simply what *is*; of saying *what* this *is*, that a thing *is*.[80]

71

Heidegger's hand is tied to the terrestrial order. Thus, it does not grasp the human future. Human beings have long since stopped dwelling between 'earth' and 'sky'. On the way towards the un-thinged [*Unbedingtheit*], they will also leave the 'mortals' and the 'divinities' behind. The *last things* (*ta eschata*) will also have to be eliminated. Human beings soar up towards the un-thinged, the unconditioned. We are headed towards a trans-human and post-human age in which human life will be a *pure exchange of information*. Human beings shed their being be-thinged, their facticity, even though this is precisely what makes them what they are. 'Human' is derived from *humus*, that is, soil. Digitalization is a resolute step along the way towards the abolition of the *humanum*. The future of humans seems mapped out: *humans will abolish themselves in order to posit themselves as the absolute.*

Things Close to the Heart

In Antoine de Saint-Exupéry's *The Little Prince*, there is a scene that illustrates the nature of things that are close to our hearts. The little prince meets a fox. He asks the fox to play with him, but the fox replies that he can't play with him because he has not been tamed by the little prince. The little prince asks him what 'taming' (*apprivoiser*) means. The fox replies:

'It is an act too often neglected', said the fox. 'It means to establish ties. . . . To me, you are still nothing more than a little boy who is just like a hundred thousand other little boys. And I have no need of you. And you,

72

on your part, have no need of me. To you, I am nothing more than a fox like a hundred thousand other foxes. But if you tame me, then we shall need each other. To me, you will be unique in all the world. To you, I shall be unique in all the world.'[81]

Intense ties are becoming less and less important. First of all, they are unproductive, for consumption and communication can be accelerated only by weak ties. For this reason, capitalism systematically destroys ties. Things that are close to our hearts are also rare today; they are increasingly being replaced by disposable items. The fox continues:

'Men have no more time to understand anything. They buy things all ready made at the shops. But there is no shop anywhere where one can buy friendship, and so men have no friends anymore.'[82]

Today, Saint-Exupéry might observe that there are indeed now shops for friends, like Facebook or Tinder.

Only after having met the fox does the little prince realize why his rose is unique for him: 'because it is she that I have sheltered behind the screen . . . because it is she that I have listened to, when she grumbled, or boasted, or even sometimes when she said nothing'.[83] The little prince makes time for his rose by 'listening' to her. *Listening* is directed at the *other*. True listeners expose themselves to the other without reservation. Without *exposure* to the other, the I raises it head again. The *metaphysical weakness for the other* is constitutive of the *ethics of listening*, which is an ethics of responsibility. The strengthening ego is incapable of listening because everywhere it hears only its own voice.

The heart beats towards the *other*. In the things close to our hearts, we also meet the *other*. Often, they are *gifts from the other*. Today, we have no time *for the other*. Time, as *time of the self*, makes us blind to the other. Intense ties, friendship and even community are brought about only by the *time of the other*. It is *good* time. Thus, the fox says:

> 'It is the time you have devoted to your rose that makes your rose so important. ... Men have forgotten this truth. ... But you must not forget it. You become responsible, forever, for what you have tamed. You are responsible for your rose.'[84]

The fox wants the little prince always to visit him at the same time – to turn the visit into a ritual. The little prince asks the fox what this ritual would be, and the fox responds: 'Those [rites] also are actions too often neglected ... They are what make one day different from other days, one hour from other hours.'[85] Rituals are temporal techniques for housing oneself.[86] They turn being-in-the-world into a being-at-home. They are to time what things are to space. They stabilize life by structuring time. They are *time architectures*. They thereby make time inhabitable; they even make time something that may be entered, like a house. Today, time lacks a solid structure. It is not a house but a wild torrent. There is nothing that gives it stability. Time that rushes off is not inhabitable.

Rituals, like things close to our hearts, are the calm centres of life; they stabilize it. They are characterized by

74

repetition. The compulsion of production and consumption eliminates repetition. It develops a compulsion of the new. Information cannot be repeated. As it is relevant only fleetingly, it reduces duration. It generates a compulsion for ever new attractions. Things close to our hearts do not have attraction. They are therefore repeatable.

The French expression *apprendre par coeur* (to learn by heart) means to appropriate by repetition. Only repetition reaches the heart. The *rhythm* of the heart is also owed to repetition. A life that has been evacuated of all repetition is without rhythm, without metre [*Takt*]. Rhythm also stabilizes the psyche. It gives time, which is by itself an unstable element, a form: 'Rhythm is the successful creation of form under the (aggravating) condition of temporality.'[87] In the age of unrepeatable emotion, affect and event, life loses form and rhythm. It becomes radically fleeting.

The time of things close to one's heart has passed. The heart belongs to the terrestrial order. Above the front door of Heidegger's house we find a verse from the Bible: 'Keep thy heart with all diligence; for out of it *are* the issues of life.'[88] Saint-Exupéry also invokes the power of the heart that brings forth *life*. When saying their farewells, the fox tells the little prince a secret to remember: 'It is only with the heart that one can see rightly; what is essential is invisible to the eye.'[89]

Stillness

The divine is an *event of stillness*. It lets us *listen*: 'The verb *myein*, "to initiate", means etymologically, "to close" – notably the eyes but, more importantly, the mouth. At the beginning of the sacred rites, the herald would "command silence" (*epitattei ten siopen*).'[1] We live in a *time without consecration*. The fundamental verb of our time is not 'to close' but *to open* – 'the eyes but, more importantly, the mouth'. Hypercommunication, the noise of communication, desecrates the world, profanes it. Stillness *produces nothing*. Capitalism therefore dislikes stillness. Information capitalism produces the compulsion of communication.

Stillness sharpens our sense for the *higher order*, which, however, need not be an order of rule or power. Stillness can be extremely peaceful, even friendly and deeply delightful. A ruling power may be able to silence the subjugated, but an enforced silence is not stillness. Real stillness knows no compulsion. It does not subjugate; it elevates. It does not take away, but gives.

For Cézanne, the task of the painter is *to establish silence*. The Montagne Sainte-Victoire appears to him as a *rising massif of stillness* that he must *obey*. The vertical, the rising, demands stillness. Cézanne creates stillness by withdrawing and becoming *no one*. He becomes a listener: 'His only aspiration must be to silence. He must stifle within himself the voices of prejudice, he must forget, always forget, establish silence, be a perfect echo. Then the landscape will inscribe itself on his sensitive tablet.'[2]

Listening is the religious gesture par excellence. Hölderlin's Hyperion says:

> My whole being stills and listens when the gentle ripple of the breeze plays about my breast. Often, lost in the immensity of blue, I look up into the aether and out into the hallowed sea, and it's as if a kindred spirit opened its arms to me, as if the pain of isolation were dissolved in the life of the godhead.
>
> To be one with everything, that is the life of the godhead, that is the heaven of man.
>
> To be one with everything that lives, to return in blissful self-oblivion into the all of nature, that is the summit of thoughts and joys, that is the holy mountain pinnacle, the place of eternal peace.[3]

We are no longer familiar with that *divine falling silent* that elevates us to the life of the godhead, to the heaven of man. Blissful self-oblivion has given way to the excessive self-production of the ego. Digital hypercommunication, unlimited connectedness, does not bring about attachment or a world. Rather, it effects isolation, deepens loneliness. The isolated, worldless, depressive I moves away from that delightful all-embracing unity, that holy mountain pinnacle.

We have abolished all transcendence, all vertical order, that demands stillness. The vertical gives way to the horizontal. Nothing *rises*. Nothing *becomes deeper*. Reality is flattened out into information and data streams. Everything sprawls and proliferates. Stillness is a phenomenon of negativity. It is *exclusive*, whereas noise is the result of permissive, extensive, excessive communication.

Stillness emanates from what is unavailable. What is not available stabilizes and deepens our attention; it brings forth a contemplative gaze. That gaze has the patience needed to see the *long-lasting* and *slow*. When everything is available and accessible, attention remains shallow. The gaze does not linger. Like that of a hunter, it wanders.

For Nicolas Malebranche, attentiveness is the natural prayer of the soul. Today, the soul no longer *prays*. It *produces itself*. Extensive communication *distracts* the soul. Only those activities that resemble prayer go together with stillness. Contemplation, however, is opposed to production. The compulsion of production and communication destroys contemplative immersion.

According to Roland Barthes, photography 'must be silent'. He does not like 'blustering photographs'. He holds that, 'in order to see a photograph well, it is best to look away or close your eyes'.[4] The *punctum*, even the *truth*, of photography reveals itself in silence, when one closes one's eyes. The information tracked by the *studium* is blustering. It imposes itself on our perception. The imagination is set in motion only by silence, by closing our eyes. Barthes quotes Kafka: 'We photograph things in order to drive them out of our minds. My stories are a way of shutting my eyes.'[5]

Without *imagination*, there is only *pornography*. Today, perception itself has something pornographic about it. It has the form of immediate contact, almost of a copulation of image and eye. The *erotic* takes place when we close our eyes. Only stillness, the imagination, discloses subjectivity's deep inward spaces of *desire*:

> Absolute subjectivity is achieved only in a state, an effort, of silence (shutting your eyes is to make the image speak in silence). The photograph touches me if I withdraw it from its usual blah-blah: . . . to say nothing, to shut my eyes.[6]

What is so ruinous about digital communication is that it means we no longer have time to close our eyes. The eyes are forced into a 'continuous voracity'.[7] They lose the capacity for stillness, for deep attentiveness. The soul no longer *prays*.

Noise is a visual as well as an acoustic filth. It pollutes the attention. Michel Serres derives the pollution of the world from the animal's will to appropriate:

> Tigers piss on the edge of their lair. And so do lions and dogs. Like those carnivorous mammals, many animals, our cousins, *mark* their territory with their harsh, stinking urine or their howling, while others such as finches and nightingales use sweet songs.[8]

We spit in the soup so that we may have it all to ourselves. The world is polluted not only by excretions and material waste but also by junk communication and information. It is plastered with advertisements. Everything is crying out for attention on a

> planet completely covered with garbage and billboards . . . On each mountain rock, each tree leaf, each agricultural plot of land, you have advertisements; letters are written on each blade of grass . . . Like the legendary cathedral, the landscape is swallowed by the tsunami of signs.[9]

Non-things block out things, pollute them. Junk information and communication destroy the silent landscape, the discreet language of things:

> *Imperious images and letters force us to read, while the pleading things of the world are begging our senses for meaning. The latter ask; the former command.* . . . our products already have a meaning, which is flat. They are the easier to perceive because they are less elaborate, similar to waste. Images are the waste of paintings; logos, the waste of writing; ads, the waste of vision; announcements, the residues of music. Forcing themselves on our perception, those low and facile signs clog up the landscape, which itself is more difficult, discreet, silent, and often dying because unseen by any saving perception.[10]

The digital seizure of land produces a lot of noise. The battle for territory gives way to the battle for attention. Appropriation also takes an altogether different form.

We incessantly produce information that has to be *liked* by others. Today's nightingales do not sing sweet songs in order to chase away others. Rather, they *tweet* in order to attract others. We do not spit in the soup to prevent others from enjoying it. Rather, our motto is *sharing*. We now want to *share* everything with everyone else. The result is a roaring tsunami of information.

Things and territories determine the terrestrial order. They are not noisy. The terrestrial order is still. The digital order is ruled by information. Stillness is alien to information. It contradicts the essence of information. Still information is an oxymoron. Information steals the silence by imposing itself on us and demanding our attention. Stillness is a phenomenon of attentiveness. Stillness is created only by deep attentiveness. Information, however, dissects attention.

According to Nietzsche, in a 'noble culture', people do '*not* . . . react immediately to a stimulus'. Such a culture develops 'the inhibiting, excluding instincts'. You need to 'let foreign things, new things of every type, come towards you while assuming an initial air of calm hostility'. Keeping 'all your doors wide open' and being 'constantly poised and ready to put yourself into – plunge yourself into – other things', that is, 'the inability to resist a stimulus', is destructive of the spirit. The 'inability *not* to react' is 'a pathology, a decline, a symptom of exhaustion'.[11] Total permissiveness and permeability destroy a noble culture. We are increasingly losing the 'excluding instincts', the ability to say 'no' to the advancing stimuli.

We need to distinguish between two kinds of potentiality. Positive potentiality consists in the ability to do

81

something. Negative potentiality is the ability to do *nothing*. The latter is, however, not identical with the inability to do something. It is not a negation of positive potential but a potential of its own. It enables spirit to engage in still, contemplative lingering, that is, deep attentiveness. In the absence of negative potential, we develop a destructive *hyperactivity*. We become submerged in noise. Stillness can be restored only by a strengthening of negative potentiality. But the dominant compulsion of communication, which is ultimately the compulsion to produce, intentionally destroys negative potentiality.

We constantly *produce* ourselves. This *production of self* is noisy. Creating stillness means *withdrawing*. Stillness is also a *phenomenon of namelessness*. I am not the *master of myself*, of *my name*. I am a *guest at* myself; I am only the tenant of my *name-hood*. Michel Serres creates stillness by deconstructing his name:

> It is indeed Michel Serres. Because my language and my society call it my own name, they pretend that I have the ownership of these two words. However, I know hundreds of Michels, Miguels, Mikes, or Mikhails. Similarly, there are Serreses, Sierras, Junipero Serras, all derived from a Ural-Altaic name designating a mountain. I have sometimes met exact homonyms. . . . And so, proper names sometimes mimic or repeat common names, even *place names* on occasion. Mine, for instance, quotes the Mont-Saint-Michel, in France, Italy, or Cornwall, three neatly aligned locations. We inhabit sites that are more or less prestigious. My name is Michel Serres, but it is not my own; I am just its tenant.[12]

82

The appropriation of a name, in particular, produces a lot of noise. The strengthening ego destroys the stillness. Where I step back, where I lose myself in namelessness, where I become weak, there is stillness: 'Soft, I mean aerial and volatile. Soft, white. Soft, peaceful.'[13]

Nietzsche knew that stillness goes along with the withdrawal of the I. Stillness teaches me to listen, to take note:

the genius of the heart, that makes everything loud and complacent fall silent and learn to listen, that smooths out rough souls and gives them the taste of a new desire, – to lie still, like a mirror that the deep sky can mirror itself upon ... the genius of the heart, that enriches everyone who has come into contact with it ... [making everyone] perhaps less certain, more gentle, fragile, and broken.[14]

Nietzsche's 'genius of the heart' does not *produce itself*. Rather, it withdraws into *namelessness*. As a will to power, the will to appropriate retreats. Power turns into *friendliness*. The 'genius of the heart' discovers the *strength in weakness* that finds expression in the *splendour of stillness*.

Only in stillness, in the *great silence*, do we enter into a relation with the *nameless*, which exceeds us and in the face of which our efforts at appropriating the name seem feeble. The genius 'who becomes each man's guardian at the moment of birth' also rises above the name.[15] The genius makes life more than the miserable survival of the I. He represents a timeless present:

Genius' youthful face and long, fluttering wings signify that he does not know time ... That is why a birthday

83

cannot be the commemoration of a past day but, like every true celebration, must be an abolition of time – the epiphany and presence of Genius. This inescapable presence prevents us from enclosing ourselves within a substantial identity and shatters the ego's pretension to be sufficient unto itself.[16]

Absolutely silent perception resembles a photograph taken with a very long exposure. Daguerre's photograph *Boulevard du Temple* actually shows a very busy street in Paris, but because of the extremely long exposure, typical of daguerreotypes, all movement disappears. Only what stands *still* is visible. *Boulevard du Temple* exudes an almost rural calmness. Apart from buildings and trees, only one human figure is recognizable, a man who is standing still to have his shoes cleaned. Perception of the long-lasting and slow thus recognizes only still things. Everything that rushes is condemned to disappear. *Boulevard du Temple* can be interpreted as a world seen through divine eyes. Only those who linger in contemplative calmness appear to God's redeeming gaze. *Stillness redeems.*

Excursus on the Jukebox

Early one evening in the autumn of 2017, I was riding my bicycle through the Schöneberg area of Berlin when there was a sudden, heavy downpour. Cycling too fast down the slightly sloping Crellestraße, I skidded and was thrown to the ground. As I slowly got to my feet, not without difficulty, I found that I was in front of a shop selling jukeboxes. Having been familiar with jukeboxes only from literature and films, I was curious, and I entered the shop. The elderly owners seemed a little surprised by my visit. Apparently, it was rare for someone to end up in their shop. I felt somewhat as though I were in a dream. Among the shop's many old objects and props, I somehow felt as if I had fallen out of time. It was probably also my painful fall that had made my perception hover. The fall created a rift in time; I time travelled into the *world of things*.

I was charmed by the jukeboxes. I went from one to the other, as if in a fairy-tale world of wonderful things. The shop was called Jukeland. The things in it shone with an alien beauty. A turquoise jukebox made by AM1, in particular, caught my attention. It was a model from the fifties. In that 'silver age' of jukeboxes, they were designed to mimic certain stylistic features of automobiles, such as fins, panorama windows or rear lights. Today, they thus look almost like the chrome-covered cars of the 1950s. I immediately fell in love with this turquoise-coloured jukebox with a large panorama window. I was determined *to own it*.

At that time, I lived in a flat that contained only an old grand piano and a metal desk from a doctor's surgery. I needed to be in an empty flat. Neither the grand piano nor the desk detracted from the emptiness; they even intensified it. Alongside them, I was a third thing. To be a still, nameless thing in space, that would mean redemption. Emptiness does not mean that there is a space with nothing in it. It is an intensity, an intense presence. It is the spatial appearance of stillness. Emptiness and stillness are siblings. Nor does stillness mean that there are no sounds to be heard. Certain sounds can even emphasize it. Stillness is an *intense form of attentiveness*. Things like a desk or grand piano create stillness by attracting and structuring attention. We are surrounded by non-things, by informational distraction that fragments our attention. Even when they are noiseless, non-things thus destroy stillness.

I put the jukebox in the room with the old grand piano. At the time, I was relentlessly practising the aria of the *Goldberg Variations*, a very difficult undertaking for someone who has never taken piano lessons. At the grand piano, I felt like a child learning to write. There is something prayer-like about learning to write. It took more than two years before I was able to play the whole aria without the sheet music. Ever since, I have repeated it like a prayer. That beautiful thing, the piano, with its cover rising like a wing, became my prayer wheel.

At night, I often went into the music room and listened to the jukebox in the dark. The diffuse, multi-coloured light from the speaker grille has its full effect only in the dark. It endows the jukebox with an erotic element. The jukebox illuminates the dark with coloured lights and creates a thing magic, to which I succumbed.

The jukebox makes listening to music a highly enjoyable visual, acoustic and tactile experience. The listening is, however, very complicated and time-intensive. As my jukebox is not in constant use, it first has to be plugged in. It takes some time for the valves to warm up. After inserting the coins, I carefully press the buttons, and with a loud rattle the whole mechanism comes to life. With a buzzing noise, the record changer begins to move; its arm grabs a record and, with great precision, puts it on the turntable. Before the needle drops, a tiny brush clears the record of dust. The whole procedure resembles a magic process, a thing magic that astounds me every time.

The jukebox brings forth *thing noises*. It gives the impression that it explicitly wants to say that it is a thing. It possesses a voluminous body. Its humming comes from deep down in its belly, as if an expression of its voluptuousness. Digital sound does not make any thing noises. It is bodiless and smooth. The sound brought forth by the jukebox, from the record and valve amplifier [*Röhrenverstärker*], differs fundamentally from digital sound. It is *material* and *bodily*. The *roaring* sound [*röhrende Klang*] touches me, gives me goosebumps.

The jukebox is a proper *counterpart*. It is a *counter-body*, like the large grand piano. When I stand in front of the jukebox or play the grand piano, I think to myself: for happiness, we need a *rising counterpart*, a presence towering above us. Digitalization abolishes every *counterpart*, every *counter*. As a consequence, we lose the feeling for what bears [*das Tragende*], for what rises [*das Ragende*], even for what elevates [*das Erhebende*]. Because we lack counterparts, we constantly fall back on our own ego, and this makes us worldless, that is, depressive.

The jukebox introduced me to the alien world of 1960s and 1970s pop music. There was not a single song on the numbered cards that I knew, so to begin with I simply pressed a combination of buttons at random and let myself be transported into that alien world. Among the titles to choose from were Johnnie Ray's 'Cry', Bobby Darin's 'Dream Lover', Sam Cooke's 'Wonderful World', Glenn Miller's 'In the Mood', The Edsels's 'Rama Lama Ding Dong', Zarah Leander's 'Ich weiß es wird einmal ein Wunder geschehen', Al Martino's 'Here in My Heart', The Crystals's 'Then He Kissed Me', and Paul Anka's 'Tell Me That You Love Me'. These titles gave me a vague sense that the world back then must have been somehow more romantic and dream-like than it is today.

In the middle of the jukebox is the red sign displaying the price for using it in pfennig and Deutschmark. As I am the lucky owner of the jukebox, I have access to a button that allows me to bypass the payment mechanism.

But so far I have made no use of it. The characteristic noise of the coin falling is as much a part of the jukebox as the crackling of the record. It is one of the beautiful thing noises that I would not want to miss. Especially in the age of YouTube, I like the fact that I have to pay something for the beautiful music. The coin is the ticket to an enchanted world.

Amid all my euphoria over the jukebox, I occasionally ask myself: where might my jukebox have stood throughout its life? It must have had an eventful one. It carries clearly visible marks of its history. I would love to be the teller of fate, the physiognomist of the thing world. My quiet room is perhaps not an appropriate place for the jukebox. When I sit at the desk, I occasionally sense its loneliness, its abandonment. I am frequently gripped by the feeling that I have torn the jukebox away from its place, that there is something sacrilegious about my ownership of it. But where might one place the jukebox today? Losing things, we are at the same time losing *places*. I console myself with the thought that my proprietorship has rescued the jukebox from its complete disappearance, that I have liberated it from the drudgery of having to be useful, that I have stripped it of its commodity character and turned it into a thing close to my heart.

For Peter Handke, the jukebox is not an isolated thing but a located being. It creates a spatial centre. The protagonist of his 'Essay on the Jukebox' sets off to find 'jukebox locations'.[1] Like a gravitational centre, a jukebox *gathers* and *attunes* everything around it into a *site*. It is *site-founding*. It imparts *still contours* to a site. The reader witnesses the thing's becoming a site and a world:

The jukebox stands in the bar, under the window, which is wide open after the heat of the day; likewise open, the door leading out to the tracks. Otherwise, the place is almost entirely without furniture; what little there is has been shoved to one side, and they are mopping up already. The lights of the jukebox are reflected in the wet terrazzo floor, a glow that gradually disappears as the floor dries. The face of the barmaid appears very pale at the window, in contrast to those of the few passengers waiting outside, which are tanned. After the departure of the Trieste–Venice Express, the building appears empty, except that on a bench two adolescent boys are tussling, yelling at the top of their voices; the railroad station is their playground at the moment. From the darkness of the pines of the karst, swarms of moths are issuing forth. A long, sealed freight train rattle-pounds by, the only bright spot against the outside of the cars being the little lead seals blowing behind on their cords. In the stillness that follows – it is the time between the last swallows and the first bats – the sound of the jukebox is heard.[2]

Handke explicitly calls the jukebox a *thing*. He talks of 'his favourite thing',[3] of 'a thing of stillness',[4] of 'mighty objects glowing in all the colors of the rainbow'.[5] The protagonist is convinced that there is a deep meaning to the thing, a meaning we have lost:

Was that supposed to mean that he regretted the disappearance of his jukeboxes, these objects of yesteryear, unlikely to have a second future?

No, he merely wanted to capture and acknowledge, before even he lost sight of it, what an object could mean to a person, above all what could emanate from a mere object.[6]

Things make us see a world in the first place. Where non-things destroy visibilities, things produce them. Things open up our *gaze*, a *gaze for sites*. The jukebox reveals to the protagonist figures that he would otherwise have missed. All are transformed – animals as well as humans – into the *dwellers*, into the *settlers of the site*. There emerges a *still life of the site*, in which everything neighbours everything else and which is framed by a *community* of *still things*:

> Suddenly figures, previously overlooked, appear all over the scene. On the bench by the box tree, a man is sleeping. On the grass behind the restroom, soldiers are stretched out, a whole group, without a trace of luggage. On the platform to Udine, leaning against a pillar, a huge black man, likewise without luggage, just in shirt and pants, engrossed in a book. From the thicket of pines behind the station swoop again and again, one following close upon another, a pair of doves. It is as if all of them were not travelers but inhabitants or settlers in the area around the railroad station.[7]

The site settlers are 'without luggage'. They are not travelling. They are *lingering*. The jukebox, as a thing, emanates the *magic of lingering*.

Handke points out that a jukebox imparts an intense presence, a *presentness*, to everything around it. Near a jukebox, everything ordinary becomes an *occurrence of presentness*. From the thing emanates a gravity that condenses and deepens fleeting phenomena around *presentness*. The creation of *presentness*, the amplified, intense presence, constitutes the *thing magic*:

> With his favorite thing there, anything else around acquired a presentness all its own. Whenever possible, he would find a seat in such joints from which he could see the entire room and a bit of the outside. Here he would often achieve, in consort with the jukebox, along with letting his imagination roam, and without engaging in the observing he found so distasteful, a strengthening of himself, or an immersion in the present, which applied to the other sights as well. And what became present about them was not so much their striking features or their particular attractions as their ordinary aspects, even just the familiar forms or colors, and such enhanced presentness seemed valuable to him – nothing more precious or more worthy of being passed on than this . . . So it *meant* something, quite simply, when a man left, a branch stirred, the bus was yellow and turned off at the station, the intersection formed a triangle, the chalk was lying at the edge of the pool table, it was raining, and, and, and.[8]

The magic of the jukebox is that it imparts presence, presentness and intensity to trivial, trifling, ordinary, customary, or fleeting matters. The thing intensifies *being*. Fleeting perceptions are given 'joints', so to speak, even bones or a scaffold. They thereby gain duration.

Another jukebox is described as a special spatial event. The protagonist comes across it in a lower ground-floor bar in a side street of the Calle Cervantes in Linares.

The bar is no bigger than a storeroom, but the jukebox performs a *spatial miracle*. Its sounds widen the room. It is part of the essence of the thing that it creates *space*:

> The proprietor, an old man (turning on the ceiling light only when a guest arrived), usually alone with the jukebox. This one had the unusual feature that all the selection tabs were blank, like nameplates in a high rise apartment house with all the names missing; like the entire place, it seemed to be out of service; only the alphanumeric codes at the beginning of the blank tabs. But all over the wall, in every direction, up to the ceiling, record covers were tacked, with the proper codes writ- ten on them by hand, and thus, after the machine had been switched on, each time only on request, the desired record – the belly of the seemingly disemboweled object turned out to be chock-full of them – could be set in motion. Suddenly there was so much space in that little hovel from the monotonous thumping deep inside the steel, so much peace emanated from that place, in the midst of the hectic Spanish pace and his own.[9]

I can follow Heidegger's critique of technology only up to a certain point. Heidegger would certainly not have wanted to include the jukebox in his collection of things. His examples of things are mirror and clasp [*Spiegel und Spange*], book and picture [*Buch und Bild*], crown and cross [*Krone und Kreuz*]. The alliteration suggests harmony among things. Technical apparatuses do not belong in Heidegger's collection of things. Even the alliteration between jewel and jukebox would not suffice to award the latter the status of a thing. There is a magical side to technology. Metallurgy, too, which was the first subject I studied, seemed like alchemy to me. It is no coincidence that Novalis studied mining and mineralogy. In his *Heinrich von Ofterdingen*, the protagonist feels in the shafts a 'wonderful delight in things which perhaps have an intimate relation to our secret being'.[10]

The jukebox is an automaton. It is part of a long tradition of musical automatons. The romantics were fascinated by automatons. There is a story by E. T. A. Hoffmann called 'Automata'. The protagonist is a mechanical puppet, a Turk who serves as an oracle. He provides answers to all questions:

> These were sometimes cold and severe, while occasionally they were sparkling and witty – even broadly so at times; at others they evinced strong sense and deep astuteness, and in some instances they were to a high degree painful and tragic. But they were always strikingly apposite to the character and affairs of the questioner.[11]

Amazon's Alexa is not an automaton but an informaton. It lacks the magic of the thing. It is quite possible that advances in artificial intelligence will soon allow it to serve as an oracle, but only as an algorithmic *computing* oracle. And this lacks magic. When everything is computable, happiness disappears. Happiness is an *occurrence* that eludes all computation. There is a profound connection between magic and happiness.[12] Computable, optimized life knows no magic, that is, no happiness.

Because it is from the 'silver age' of jukeboxes, half of my jukebox is made of metal. It has a really beautiful body.

Metals are a fascinating material. For many years, I studied their secret inner life. When I studied metallurgy, I often noticed that metals behave like living organisms. They are, for instance, highly transformative. One could write a treatise about the *Metamorphosis* of metals too.[13] Among all the books of philosophy on my bookshelves stands a book by Paul G. Shewmon, *Transformations in Metals*. It is the last book I read before I decided to drop metallurgy for philosophy. I keep it as a memento. Had I read it as an e-book, I would own one less thing that is close to my heart, that I can pick up again to remind myself of past times. Things make time graspable, and rituals make time something one may enter, like a house. The book's yellowed pages and its smell warm my heart. Digitalization destroys recollection and touch.

The belief that matter is not alive is probably incorrect. I am fascinated by matter. We are today completely blind to the *magic of matter*. The digital de-materialization of the world is painful for lovers of matter. I agree with Barthes when he says that every metal of alchemy is alive. The 'prodigious idea of Nonorganic Life', Deleuze and Guattari write in *A Thousand Plateaus*, was 'the intuition of metallurgy'. To a metallurgist, everything appears alive.[14] Metallurgists are *romantics*, 'itinerants because they follow the matter-flow of the subsoil'.[15] On metallurgy and alchemy, Deleuze and Guattari write:

> The relation between metallurgy and alchemy reposes not, as Jung believed, on the symbolic value of metal and its correspondence with an organic soul but on the immanent power of corporeality in all matter, and on the esprit de corps accompanying it.[16]

95

In the course of digitalization, we have lost any awareness of materiality. A re-romanticization of the world would presuppose its re-materialization. We exploit the world with such brutality because we have declared matter to be something dead and the earth to be a mere resource. If we are to thoroughly and fundamentally revise the way we treat the earth, sustainability alone will not be enough. What is needed is an *altogether different understanding of the earth and of matter*. The American philosopher Jane Bennett, in her book *Vibrant Matter*, sets out from the assumption 'that the image of dead or thoroughly instrumentalized matter feeds human hubris and our earth-destroying fantasies of conquest and consumption'.[17] Thus, ecology must be preceded by a new ontology of matter, one that views it as something that lives. The music of the jukebox, like Barthes's photography, is an *ectoplasm*, an *emanation* of the referent. This music has something to do with resurrection. The dead, brought back to life, enter the revolving stage. I wanted to use the jukebox to bring back to life the French singer Barbara in particular. I loved her very much. Some years ago, I intended to make a film about her, so on the twentieth anniversary of her death, I took my camera and went to Paris. I made recordings while walking through Paris and singing Barbara songs. I passed her house in Rue Vitruve, stood in front of her grave in the cemetery of Bagneux, and walked over the Pont Neuf. The jukebox makes Barbara a corporeal presence again. It is a *medium of presence*. To me, the visible grooves of the record are like traces of her body. They are the vibrations that emanated from her delicate body.

I bought Barbara's jukebox records from all over

96

Europe. The sellers always turned out to be lovers of things. A man from Belgium, from whom I bought 'Dis, quand reviendras-tu?', put thirty beautiful old Belgian stamps on the parcel, thus making it a beautiful thing. I even recognized one of the stamps. It had been part of my childhood collection.

The package from Belgium found its place in a drawer, next to other beautiful things: an old, delicately engraved pocket watch that I bought thirty-five years ago while studying in Freiburg; a silver Junghans wrist-watch a friend bought for me (he wears the same sort); a Jugendstil magnifying glass that I use when reading my old leather-clasped Luther Bible; a small portable ashtray with a knitted rose on it; a cigarette case in art deco style that I received as a birthday present many years ago; and a wooden stamp with the three Chinese signs for my name. The last was made out of a special piece of wood by a Korean stamp maker. It is made from the wood of a date palm that was struck by lightning. It is said to possess magic powers and to ward off misfortune. The stamp maker also gave me a few small separate pieces of the wood before I left. I keep one of them in my purse. That little wooden thing is my amulet.

It used to be customary in Japan for people to bid farewell to things that they had used for a long time, such as spectacles or quills, by performing a ceremony in the temple. Today, there are probably very few things to which we would grant such an honourable farewell. Things now come into the world almost stillborn. They are not used but used up. Things get a soul only through long use. Only things that are close to the heart are animated. Flaubert wanted to be buried with his inkwell.

The jukebox, however, is presumably too large to be taken to the grave. My jukebox is, I believe, the same age as I, but it will certainly survive me. There is some comfort in that . . .

NOTES

Preface
1 Yoko Ogawa, *The Memory Police*, London: Vintage, 2020.

From Things to Non-things
1 Hannah Arendt, *The Human Condition*, Chicago: Chicago University Press, 1998 [1958], p. 137.
2 Vilém Flusser, *Dinge und Undinge: Phänomenologische Skizzen*, Munich: Hanser, 1993, p. 81.
3 Arendt, *The Human Condition*, p. 137.
4 Niklas Luhmann, *Entscheidungen in der 'Informations-gesellschaft'*, https://www.fen.ch/texte/gast_luhmann_info rmationsgesellschaft.htm.
5 There has been an increasing interest in things in cultural studies over the past few decades. This theoretical interest in things, however, does not mean that things are becoming more important in everyday life. On the contrary, the fact that they have become the explicit

99

subject of theoretical reflection is a sign that they are disappearing. The song of praise for things is in fact their swan song. Banned from the lifeworld, they seek refuge in theory. Similarly, 'material culture' and the 'material turn' can be understood as reactions to the de-materialization and de-reification of reality brought about by digitalization.

6 Jean Baudrillard, *Das Andere selbst: Habilitation*, Vienna: Edition Passagen, 1994, p. 11.

7 Luciano Floridi, *The Fourth Revolution: How the Infosphere is Reshaping Human Reality*, Oxford: Oxford University Press, 2014, pp. 94ff.

8 Eric Schmidt and Jared Cohen, *The New Digital Age: Reshaping the Future of People, Nations, and Business*, New York: Alfred A. Knopf, 2013, pp. 29–31. 'Your apartment is an electronic orchestra, and you are the conductor. With simple flicks of the wrist and spoken instructions, you can control temperature, humidity, ambient music and lighting. You are able to skim through the day's news on translucent screens while a freshly cleaned suit is retrieved from your automated closet because your calendar indicates an important meeting today. . . . Your central computer system suggests a list of chores your housekeeping robots should tackle today, all of which you approve. . . . There's a bit of time left before you need to leave for work – which you'll get to by driverless car, of course. Your car knows what time you need to be in the office each morning based on your calendar and, after factoring in traffic data, it communicates with your wristwatch to give you a sixty-minute countdown to when you need to leave the house. . . . Perhaps you grab an apple on the way out, to eat in the backseat of your car as it chauffeurs you to your office.'

9 Hannah Arendt, 'Truth and Politics', in *Between Past and*

Future: Eight Exercises in Political Thought, New York: Viking Press, 1968 [1954], pp. 227–64; here: p. 264.

10 Georg Friedrich Wilhelm Hegel, *Jenaer Systementwürfe III* (Naturphilosophie und Philosophie des Geistes), Hamburg: Meiner, 1987, pp. 189f.

11 Vilém Flusser, *Medienkultur*, Frankfurt am Main: Fischer, 1997, p. 187.

12 Flusser, *Dinge und Undinge*, p. 84.

13 Friedrich Nietzsche, *Thus Spoke Zarathustra*, Cambridge: Cambridge University Press, 2006, p. 10.

14 Flusser, *Dinge und Undinge*, pp. 87f.

From Possessing to Experiencing

1 Erich Fromm, *To Have or To Be*, London and New York: Continuum, 1997 [1976], p. 71.

2 Jeremy Rifkin, *The Age of Access: The New Culture of Hypercapitalism, Where All of Life is a Paid-For Experience*, New York: Jeremy P. Tarcher/Putnam, 2000, p. 7. [Transl. note: the first sentence is taken from the cover of the German edition and is not part of the original American edition.]

3 Flusser, *Dinge und Undinge*, p. 82.

4 Walter Benjamin, 'Unpacking My Library', in *Illuminations*, London: Pimlico, 1999, pp. 61–9; here: p. 69.

5 Walter Benjamin, 'Paris, the Capital of the Nineteenth Century (1935)', in *The Arcades Project*, Cambridge MA: Harvard University Press, 1999, pp. 3–13; here: p. 9.

6 Ibid.

7 Benjamin, 'Unpacking My Library', p. 62.

8 Ibid.

9 Ibid.

Smartphone

1 Walter Benjamin, *Berlin Childhood around 1900*, Cambridge MA: Harvard University Press, 2006, pp. 49f.
2 Ibid., p. 48.
3 Roland Barthes, *Mythologies*, New York: Farrar, Straus & Giroux, 1972, p. 90.
4 Martin Heidegger, 'The Age of the World Picture', in *Off the Beaten Track*, Cambridge: Cambridge University Press, 2002, p. 67 (emph. B.-Ch. H.).
5 Ernst Troeltsch, 'Epochen und Typen der Sozialphilosophie des Christentums', in *Gesammelte Schriften*, vol. 4: *Aufsätze zur Geistesgeschichte und Religionssoziologie*, Tübingen: Mohr, 1925, pp. 122–55; here: p. 134.
6 Ibid., p. 135.
7 Shoshana Zuboff, *The Age of Surveillance Capitalism: The Fight for a Human Future at the New Frontier of Power*, London: Profile Books, 2019, p. 525.
8 Donald Winnicott, *Playing and Reality*, London: Routledge, 1991, p. 2.
9 Tilmann Habermas, *Geliebte Objekte: Symbole und Instrumente der Identitätsbildung*, Berlin and New York: De Gruyter, 1996, p. 325.
10 Ibid., p. 336.
11 Ibid., p. 337.

Selfies

1 Roland Barthes, *Camera Lucida: Reflections on Photography*, London: Vintage, 2000, p. 93.
2 Ibid., pp. 87, 88, 81.
3 Ibid., p. 82.
4 Ibid.
5 Giorgio Agamben, *Profanations*, New York: Zone Books, 2007, p. 27.
6 Ibid., p. 26 (transl. modified).

7   Ibid., p. 25.

8   Barthes, *Camera Lucida*, p. 87.

9   Ibid., p. 80.

10 Wim Wenders, *Landschaften. Photograpien*, Düsseldorf: Schirmer Mosel, 2015, p. 229.

11 Ibid., p. 84.

12 Walter Benjamin, 'The Work of Art in the Age of Its Technological Reproducibility', in *The Work of Art in the Age of Its Technological Reproducibility and Other Writings on Media*, Cambridge MA: Harvard University Press, 2008, p. 27 (transl. modified).

Artificial Intelligence

1   Hubert L. Dreyfus, *What Computers Can't Do: A Critique of Artificial Intelligence*, New York: Harper & Row, 1972, p. 186.

2   Martin Heidegger, *Being and Time*, Oxford: Blackwell, 1962, p. 176. [Transl. note: Heidegger's terms *Stimmung*, *stimmen*, *Gestimmtheit* are variably translated as 'mood', 'attunement', 'tuning' or 'basic disposition'. The different translations have been retained in quotations, while 'attunement' is used outside of quotations.]

3   Martin Heidegger, *The Fundamental Concepts of Metaphysics: World, Finitude, Solitude*, Bloomington: Indiana University Press, 1995, p. 132.

4   Martin Heidegger, *Contributions to Philosophy (Of the Event)*, Bloomington: Indiana University Press, 2012, p. 19.

5   Martin Heidegger, *What Is Philosophy?*, Lanham: Rowman & Littlefield, 1958, p. 77 (transl. amended).

6   Heidegger, *The Fundamental Concepts of Metaphysics*, pp. 57, 69.

7   Heidegger, *Contributions to Philosophy (Of the Event)*, p. 19.

8 Heidegger, *What Is Philosophy?*, pp. 87/89 (transl. amended).

9 Martin Heidegger, *What Is Called Thinking?*, New York: Harper & Row, 1968, p. 207.

10 Martin Heidegger, *Hölderlin's Hymn 'The Ister'*, Bloomington: Indiana University Press, 1996, pp. 107f.

11 Dreyfus, *What Computers Can't Do*, pp. 189ff.

12 Georg Friedrich Wilhelm Hegel, *Encyclopedia of the Philosophical Sciences in Basic Outline, Part I: Science of Logic*, Cambridge: Cambridge University Press, 2010, p. 229.

13 Ibid.

14 Ibid., p. 242.

15 Ibid., p. 254.

16 Georg Friedrich Wilhelm Hegel, *The Science of Logic*, Cambridge: Cambridge University Press, 2010, p. 588.

17 Martin Heidegger, 'Logos (Heraclitus, Fragment B 50)', in *Early Greek Thinking: The Dawn of Western Philosophy*, New York: Harper & Row, 1975, pp. 59–78; here: p. 78.

18 Martin Heidegger, Letter of 14 February 1950, in *Letters to His Wife (1915–1970)*, Cambridge: Polity, 2008, p. 213.

19 www2.univ-paris8.fr/deleuze/article.php3?id_article=131 (last accessed: 10 June 2021).

20 Gilles Deleuze and Félix Guattari, *What Is Philosophy?*, New York: Columbia University Press, 1994, p. 62.

Views of Things

1 Francis Ponge, *Schreibpraktiken oder Die stetige Unfertigkeit*, Munich: Hanser, 1988, p. 69; Francis Ponge, *Pratiques d'écriture ou L'inachèvement perpétuel*, Paris: Éditions Hermann, 1984.

2 Jacques Derrida, *Signéponge/Signsponge*, New York: Columbia University Press, 1984, pp. 13/12.

3 See Matthew B. Crawford, *The World beyond Your Head: On Becoming an Individual in an Age of Distraction*, New York: Farrar, Straus and Giroux, 2015, pp. 70ff.

4 See Dorothee Kimmich, *Lebendige Dinge in der Moderne*, Konstanz: Konstanz University Press, 2011, p. 92.

5 Ernst Bloch, 'The Reverse of Things', in *Traces*, Stanford: Stanford University Press, 2006, pp. 134–6; here: p. 136.

6 Ibid., p. 135.

7 Ibid., pp. 134f.

8 Friedrich Theodor Vischer, *Auch Einer: Eine Reisebekanntschaft*, vol. 1, Stuttgart and Leipzig: Hallberger, 1879, pp. 32f.

9 Robert Musil, *The Confusions of Young Törless*, Oxford: Oxford University Press, 2014, pp. 103f. (transl. modified).

10 Jean-Paul Sartre, *Nausea*, New York: New Directions, 2007, p. 10.

11 Jean-Paul Sartre, *Being and Nothingness: A Phenomenological Essay on Ontology*, New York: Washington Square Press, 1966, p. 346.

12 Rainer Maria Rilke, *Diaries of a Young Poet*, New York: W. W. Norton, 1998, p. 88.

13 Walter Benjamin, 'One-Way-Street', in *One-Way-Street and Other Writings*, London: NLB, 1979, pp. 45–104; here: p. 58.

14 Martin Buber, *I and Thou*, Edinburgh: T. & T. Clark, 1937, p. 4.

15 Franz Kafka, 'The Cares of a Family Man', in *Collected Stories*, London: David Campbell Publishers, pp. 183–5; here: 183.

16 Ibid., p. 184.

17 Ibid.

18 Ibid., p. 185.

19 Franz Kafka, *Letters to Milena*, New York: Schocken Books, 1990, p. 223 (all subsequent quotations from this text: ibid.).

20 Kafka, 'The Cares of a Family Man', p. 184.

21 Gumbrecht rightly points out 'the tendency in contemporary culture to abandon and even forget the possibility of a presence-based relationship to the world'. Hans Ulrich Gumbrecht, *Production of Presence: What Meaning Cannot Convey*, Stanford: Stanford University Press, 2004, pp. xivf.

22 Hugo von Hofmannsthal, 'Eine Monographie', in *Gesammelte Werke: Reden und Aufsätze* I, pp. 479–83; here: p. 479.

23 Hugo von Hofmannsthal, 'The Letter of Lord Chandos', in *Selected Prose*, New York: Pantheon Books, 1952, pp. 129–41; here: p. 137.

24 Ibid., p. 136.

25 Ibid., p. 140.

26 Ibid., p. 139.

27 Ibid., p. 137.

28 Ibid., p. 138.

29 Ibid., p. 140.

30 Ibid., p. 141 (transl. amended).

31 Barthes, *Camera Lucida*, p. 27.

32 Ibid., p. 26.

33 Ibid., pp. 51/53.

34 Ibid., p. 26.

35 Ibid., p. 27.

36 See ibid., pp. 40ff.

37 Ibid., p. 41.

38 Ibid., p. 57.

39 Sigmund Freud, 'Project for a Scientific Psychology', in

Standard Edition, vol. 1, London: The Hogarth Press and the Institute of Psychoanalysis, 1966, pp. 283–397; here: p. 331.

40 Jacques Lacan, *The Ethics of Psychoanalysis (1959–1960)*, New York: W. W. Norton, 1992, p. 46.

41 See ibid., pp. 134–6.

42 Barthes, *Camera Lucida*, p. 59.

43 Rainer Maria Rilke, *The Letters of Rainer Maria Rilke*, New York: W. W. Norton, 1945, p. 124.

44 Roland Barthes, *The Pleasures of the Text*, New York: Hill and Wang, 1998, p. 10.

45 Robert Walser, *Briefe*, Zurich: Suhrkamp, 1979, p. 266.

46 Ponge, *Schreibpraktiken*, p. 82. 'À partir du moment où l'on considère les mots (et les expressions verbales) comme une matière, il est très agréable de s'en occuper. Tout autant que peut l'être pour un peintre de s'occuper des couleurs et des formes. Très plaisant d'en jouer.' Ponge, *Pratiques d'écriture*, p. 89.

47 Ponge, *Schreibpraktiken*, p. 13. 'Pour pouvoir en tirer une jouissance en dehors de leur signification autant que possible. Je tâche à les éloigner de moi pour m'en libérer et pour m'en venger et pour y trouver un noveau monde, un nouveau lieu d'exercices et de plaisirs.' Ponge, *Pratiques d'écriture*, p. 18.

48 Roland Barthes, 'The Grain of the Voice', in *Image – Music – Text*, London: Fontana Press, 1977, pp. 179–89; here: p. 182.

49 Ibid., pp. 181f. (transl. modified).

50 Ibid., p. 182.

51 Ibid., p. 184.

52 Maurice Merleau-Ponty, 'Cézanne's Doubt', in *Sense and Non-Sense*, Evanston: Northwestern University Press, 1964, pp. 9–25; here: p. 19 (transl. amended).

53 The politicization of art contributes a great deal to

its disenchantment. See Robert Pfaller, *Die blitzenden Waffen: Über die Macht der Form*, Frankfurt am Main: S. Fischer, 2020, p. 93.

54 John Berger, *Ways of Seeing*, London: BBC and Penguin, 1972, p. 31.

55 Jean Baudrillard, *Seduction*, Montreal: New World Perspectives and CTheory Books, 2001, p. 79.

56 Ibid., p. 80.

57 According to Hannah Arendt: *Hannah Arendt – Martin Heidegger: Letters 1925–1975*, Orlando: Harcourt, 2004, p. 154.

58 Heidegger, *What is Called Thinking?*, p. 16 (transl. amended).

59 Martin Heidegger, *Parmenides*, Bloomington: Indiana University Press, 1998, p. 85.

60 Ibid., p. 81.

61 Ibid.

62 Ibid.

63 Ibid., p. 85.

64 Martin Heidegger, 'Johann Peter Hebel', in *Reden und andere Zeugnisse eines Lebensweges, 1910–1976*, *Gesamtausgabe*, vol. 16, Frankfurt am Main: Klostermann, 2000, pp. 530–3; here: p. 532.

65 Martin Heidegger, 'Anaximander's Saying (1946)', in *Off the Beaten Track*, Cambridge: Cambridge University Press, 2002, pp. 242–81; here: p. 260.

66 Heidegger, *Being and Time*, p. 98.

67 Martin Heidegger, 'The Origin of the Work of Art', in *Off the Beaten Track*, pp. 1–56; here: p. 14.

68 Ibid., p. 13.

69 Ibid., pp. 13f.

70 Ibid., p. 14.

71 Ibid., p. 15.

72 Martin Heidegger, 'The Pathway', in *Heidegger: The*

Man and the Thinker, ed. Thomas Sheehan, Chicago: Precedent Publishing, 1981, pp. 69–71; here: p. 71 (transl. amended). Note that the text is not included in the book's table of contents.

73 Martin Heidegger, 'The Thing', in *Poetry, Language, Thought*, New York: Harper & Row, 1971, pp. 164–84; here: p. 178.

74 Ibid., p. 177.

75 Ibid., p. 180.

76 Heidegger, 'Anaximander's Saying (1946)', p. 276 (transl. amended).

77 Martin Heidegger, 'Why Poets?', in *Off the Beaten Track*, pp. 200–41; here: pp. 223f.

78 Heidegger, 'The Thing', p. 179.

79 Martin Heidegger, 'The Question Concerning Technology', in *The Question Concerning Technology and Other Essays*, New York: Garland Publishing, 1977, pp. 3–35; here: p. 23.

80 Heidegger, 'Anaximander's Saying (1946)', pp. 280f.

81 Antoine de Saint-Exupéry, *The Little Prince*, Boston: G. K. Hall & Co., 1995, pp. 128ff.

82 Ibid., p. 133.

83 Ibid., pp. 138f.

84 Ibid., pp. 139f.

85 Ibid., pp. 134ff.

86 See Antoine de Saint-Exupéry, *The Wisdom of the Sands*, New York: Harcourt Bracc, 1950, pp. 15f.

87 Hans Ulrich Gumbrecht, 'Rhythmus und Sinn', in Hans Ulrich Gumbrecht and Karl Ludwig Pfeiffer (eds), *Materialität der Kommunikation*, Frankfurt am Main: Suhrkamp, 1988, pp. 714–29; here: p. 717.

88 Proverbs 4:23.

89 Saint-Exupéry, *The Little Prince*, p. 139.

Stillness

1 Giorgio Agamben and Monica Ferrando, *The Unspeakable Girl: The Myth and Mystery of Kore*, London: Seagull Books, 2014, p. 10.

2 Joachim Gasquet, *Cézanne*, Paris: Bernheim-Jeune, 1931, pp. 131–3. Quoted in Theodore Reff, *Cézanne: The Late Work*, New York: Museum of Modern Art, 1977, p. 406.

3 Friedrich Hölderlin, *Hyperion, or the Hermit in Greece*, Cambridge: Open Book Publishers, 2019, p. 8.

4 Barthes, *Camera Lucida*, pp. 53ff.

5 Ibid., p. 53.

6 Ibid., p. 55.

7 Ibid.

8 Michel Serres, *Malfeasance: Appropriation through Pollution?*, Stanford: Stanford University Press, 2010, p. 1.

9 Ibid., pp. 69f.

10 Ibid., p. 51.

11 Friedrich Nietzsche, *Twilight of the Idols*, in *The Anti-Christ, Ecce Homo, Twilight of the Idols and Other Writings*, Cambridge: Cambridge University Press, 2005, pp. 153–229; here: pp. 190f.

12 Serres, *Malfeasance*, pp. 87f.

13 Ibid., p. 89.

14 Friedrich Nietzsche, *Beyond Good and Evil*, Cambridge: Cambridge University Press, 2002, p. 175.

15 Giorgio Agamben, *Profanations*, New York: Zone Books, 2007, p. 9.

16 Ibid., pp. 11f.

Excursus on the Jukebox

1 Peter Handke, 'Essay on the Jukebox', in *The Jukebox and Other Essays on Storytelling*, New York: Farrar, Straus, Giroux, 1994, pp. 47–118; here: p. 72.

2 Ibid., pp. 105f.

3 Ibid., p. 98 (transl. modified).

4 My translation, D. S. – The English translation gives 'source of peace', losing the theme of the 'thing'; see ibid., p. 89.

5 Ibid., p. 52.

6 Ibid., p. 103.

7 Ibid., p. 106 (transl. modified).

8 Ibid., pp. 98f. (transl. modified).

9 Ibid., pp. 116f.

10 Novalis (Friedrich von Hardenberg), *Henry of Ofterdingen*, Cambridge: John Owen, 1842, p. 88.

11 E. T. A. Hoffmann, 'Automata', in *The Best Tales of Hoffmann*, New York: Dover, 1967, pp. 71–103; here: p. 80.

12 Agamben, *Profanations*, pp. 19f.

13 Transl. note: An allusion to Goethe's *The Metamorphosis of Plants*.

14 Gilles Deleuze and Félix Guattari, *A Thousand Plateaus: Capitalism and Schizophrenia*, London: Bloomsbury, 2013, p. 479.

15 Ibid., p. 480.

16 Ibid., p. 479.

17 Jane Bennett, *Vibrant Matter: A Political Ecology of Things*, Durham NC: Duke University Press, 2010, p. ix.